Featuring more than thirty romantic kisses, *The Art of Kissing* is your key to romance. Even if you've never kissed before, this book will teach you so much that no one will ever know it's your first time. And experienced kissers will learn so many new secrets they'll astonish their partners. Whatever you do, read this book before your boyfriend or girlfriend does!

"Get it and expand *your* puckering portfolio."
—*Seventeen*

"You are bound to learn something new about kissing if you read this book."
—*Newtown Bee* (Newtown, Connecticut)

"*The Art of Kissing* goes beyond the valley of French kissing by exploring . . . such advanced exercises as the underwater kiss, the counterkiss, and the electric kiss (rub your stockinged feet on the carpet and *whoa!*)."
—*Washington Times*

"Whoever said 'a kiss is just a kiss' didn't get his mitts on *The Art of Kissing* . . . a

MARGARET MORGAN
and
MARY MORGAN PEDLOW
Memorial

RIVERSIDE PUBLIC LIBRARY

It's never too late to learn . . .

After reading this book a whole new you will emerge. You'll become such a passionate, exciting, romantic kisser that your dates will cry tears of pleasure. Inside, you'll discover:

♥ The newest fads in French kissing
♥ How to boost kissability
♥ Where men (and women) like being kissed best
♥ How to increase kissing compatibility
♥ How to perform today's trendiest kisses, including
 ♡ Lip-o-Suction
 ♡ The Hollywood kiss
 ♡ The Statue kiss
 ♡ The Sartrean kiss
 ♡ The Trobriand Islands kiss

As seen on TV, here's the eagerly awaited second version of the kissing bible featured on *CBS This Morning, The View,* and *The Today Show,* completely revised with new statistics, new kisses, new instructions!

detailed how-to book . . . this year's handy alternative to chocolates." —*Elle*

"It's refreshing to think about kissing per se rather than as a prelude to something else." —*Self*

"If you . . . want to smooch like Rick and Elsa in *Casablanca,* this bussing bible is for you." —Lowell (Massachusetts) *Sun*

"Some terrific tips on how you can make every kiss as passionate and thrilling as your first." —*The National Enquirer*

"I advise you to race full speed to your bookstore and pick up a copy of *The Art of Kissing* . . . it could save you emotional problems."

—*Clarion Ledger* (Jackson, Mississippi)

"*The Art of Kissing* is perhaps the most thorough encyclopedia on swapping slobber ever available. . . . Cane covers every kind of kissing imaginable. . . . Whether you're looking to improve your skills or save your hide after giving a lousy Valentine's Day gift, *The Art of Kissing* is sure to be effective." —Richardson (Texas) *News*

"The definitive book . . . lighthearted . . . fun . . . worth more than lip service!"
—Oxford (England) *Mail*

The

Art of Kissing

Also by William Cane

The Book of Kisses

The Art of Hugging

The Art of Kissing Book of Questions and Answers

The

Art of Kissing

Second Revised Edition

William Cane

St. Martin's Griffin
New York

For Carla Mayer Glasser

THE ART OF KISSING (second revised edition). Copyright ©
2005 by William Cane. All rights reserved. Printed in
China. For information, address St. Martin's Press, 175
Fifth Avenue, New York, N.Y. 10010.

www.stmartins.com

Illustrations copyright © 1995 by Durell Godfrey.

Library of Congress Cataloging-in-Publication Data

Cane, William.
    The art of kissing / William Cane.—2nd rev. ed.,
1st St. Martin's Griffin ed
        p. cm.
    ISBN 978-0-312-33497-0
        I. Title.

  GT2640.C36 2005
  394—dc22

                                        2004051164

Flexi-bound edition: ISBN 978-0-312-61580-2
Flexi-bound Revised Second Edition: January 2010

10   9   8   7   6   5   4

CONTENTS

PART THREE: HOW TO FRENCH-KISS

$\mathcal{P}$ REFACE

This book is the result of a kiss, and a rather embarrassing one at that. I had been kissing a certain young woman when she broke off and pushed away, her mouth a gaping oval of surprise and her blue eyes wide with shock and annoyance. I was taken aback by this sudden reversal of emotion: A moment before she had been kissing me passionately.

"You're not supposed to kiss with your eyes open," she said.

I was totally bewildered. Where in the book of kissing did it say that you had to kiss with your eyes closed? I asked her, but she couldn't tell me. "It's not nice to kiss and look," she insisted. And because she liked to kiss with her eyes closed I had to follow suit. That was her logic, and of course—being under her spell—I played by her rules.

But I was vexed, for I wanted to be able to refer to some authority to show that it was all right to kiss with your eyes open. Unfortunately the books on kissing that I consulted at the library were woefully silent on this and many other points. The best of the old books, *The Art of Kissing,* by Hugh Morris (1936), discussed a number of kisses in separate chapters, but its treatment was out-of-date and often consisted of merely a collection of quotes from classical poets. Neither Morris nor the other writers gave more than a perfunctory description of how to execute the kisses they discussed. It was as if they avoided detail on purpose.

Puzzled at the lack of explicitness in these works, I set out to obtain the information myself, gathering data through interviews, surveys, and sixteen years of research conducted in some of the most far-flung corners of the globe.

You hold in your hands the second revised edition of this book, which contains new kisses and updated statistics from a hundred thousand people. Because you asked for it, I've expanded the chapter on the French kiss into a whole new section. I've tracked down people who like to kiss and barraged them with questions until they revealed their carefully guarded kissing secrets. All of that is in this book.

My purpose was simple. I wanted to give you the best book on kissing ever written. I wanted to give you the secret to great kissing. I wanted to give you the truth about what men and women do, think, and feel when they kiss so that *you* can become a better kisser.

May this book both entertain you and inspire you to kiss.

William Cane
February 2005

PART ONE

The Psychology of Kissing

Ｗhat is kissing?

If we had to be blunt and direct we could agree with Dr. Henry Gibbons that a kiss is simply "the anatomical juxtaposition of two *orbicularis oris* muscles in a state of contraction." But who wants to be blunt and direct? The real point is, What does kissing mean? What does it do to you? How does it make you feel? To answer those questions you have to ask people who are in love or who are infatuated because they—and not dictionaries—are the true experts when it comes to defining what kissing is. Here are some of their responses.

What do you like most about kissing?

WOMEN:
"I just love to kiss. It's the biggest turn-on."

"I like the feeling of breathing someone else's space, sharing with them the basis of life, i.e., air. There's that inexplicable feeling that's like having an extreme, uncontrollable case of the shivers, but not quite, and being so close to someone that you can really smell what their scent is."

"It lowers my blood pressure, warms my mood, and suppresses my appetite for sweet things, especially chocolate. I feel intoxicated (only with the right guy) and want to kiss for a long time. It's not necessarily a prelude to sex. It's a spiritual connection, exploring and devouring. Sometimes it makes me shake, sweat, laugh uncontrollably."

"Being held close while it is happening—like I'm a fragile, precious thing."

"The thing I like most about kissing is the closeness it creates. Also you can tell a lot from a kiss. A kiss is like a window into someone's inner thoughts. You can sense the mood of the person you're kissing. You can often tell how they really feel about you from a kiss. Someone who really cares for you will not kiss you the same way as someone who is just there for sex. Another thing I like about kissing is that it always foreshadows what might be coming."

"Being able to vary it so much—French kiss, regular kiss, on the side of the mouth, biting, licking, sucking, exploring. It's never boring! And you have your hands free to touch other parts, too."

"Sexually, it's expressive . . . exciting . . . usually the first tactile contact you have with the other person. It's warming and brings you close. Nonsexually, it's affectionate, friendly."

"I like being physically close to the other person . . . the closeness, hugging, and arms intertwined, more than the actual kiss, except in unusual cases."

MEN:
"I like a violent and slightly wet mouth."

"My girlfriend's breath, the feel of her lips and tongue."

"I can't quite put my finger on it, whether it's the hunger of passion, some mystical unknown sense developed in my mouth, the soft cat-showers and massages, or being in contact with my woman's sexy mouth or legs. I'm so overwhelmed by the experience, the feelings are not simple, and they saturate my mind with pleasure."

Is there anything you don't like about kissing?

WOMEN:
"Smoker's breath!"

"Beard burn. Bad breath. When it doesn't vary at all."

"When a person isn't gentle or sensual—too deep and passionate a kiss before I'm ready for it. When a person glosses over kissing just to get to the next step."

"Being kissed with an open mouth when you only *like* the kisser."

"When people I don't know kiss me on the mouth. My brother-in-law kisses with his tongue out. Everybody hates to kiss him."

"Sometimes a man with no subtlety will thrust a pasty tongue into your mouth and it's like *oral rape!* A misfit of mouths. Or a man who has no passion in kissing. A too-delicate kisser can be irritating."

Do you ever get very aroused simply by kissing?

WOMEN:

"Definitely! It makes my mouth tingle, my head gets dizzy, my blood runs hotter through my veins."

"Yes, yes, yes, yes. I have a one-and-a-half-year friendship that includes only kissing and petting, and *boy* do I get aroused. It's amazing. Especially since I know it won't go further, it's also tantalizing."

"Arousal starts with the kiss for me. Okay, maybe it starts before that. But the kiss most definitely gets me moving along."

"Yes, if we're standing very close to each other."

"Yes. When kisses are very slow, gentle, wet, accompanied by light touches to the face and neck."

MEN:

"Positively yes."

"Ever? Always."

"Very. It's as close as you can get to anyone before it gets obscene in public. If you're Frenching it's like giving yourself to one another."

"Yes. For example a prolonged surprise kiss in the kitchen once led to kissing and cuddling on the living room floor."

What goes through your mind when you kiss?

WOMEN:

"How's he feeling? Does he really care for me? Does he like the *way* I kiss? What's going to happen if we both get out of control?"

"I like to see how turned on he gets. Usually it's as much as I do."

"It's about time he kissed me!"

"Generally it's the physical sensations I'm aware of. Mentally I'm evaluating the kissing ability of the other person, the give-and-take and the response of the other person."

MEN:
"I daydream about what it would be like if she was naked in bed. Sometimes I wonder what it would be like to be married to the person."

"I often wonder what's next. Your mind immediately starts to think about sex and intercourse."

"I'm thinking about the kiss itself: 'Am I enjoying it? *What* am I enjoying about it? What am I going to do in return?' If I'm *not* enjoying it, *that's* what I'm thinking about."

"A warm, relaxed feeling."

"How far I'll get with the girl."

"What a lucky thrill I'm getting!"

Freud said even a kiss can be considered a perversion because it's not strictly speaking necessary for procreation—it's simply oral pleasure. Adam Phillips had a more amusing definition. "Kissing," he said, "involves some of the pleasures of eating in the absence of nourishment." He's right, isn't he? Just think of eating your favorite foods . . . ice cream . . . strawberries . . . toast.

Toast?

That crunch! crunch! crunch! . . . It feels good to eat it.

And that's what kissing is—oral pleasure.

Sure, it's oral pleasure. You just have to remember—your partner is more than a baked potato. He or she has feelings too (and wants to experience pleasure just as you do).

So although we're going to investigate the physical pleasures of kissing in this book, we're also going to look at what goes through a person's heart and mind when kissing. Because kissing is more than mere technique. It's passion, romance, and above all love.

The ROMANCE
OF KISSING

It's not hard to tell when two people are in love. Maybe they're trying to hide it from the world, still they cannot conceal their inner excitement. Men will give themselves away by a certain excited trembling in the muscles of the lower jaw upon seeing their beloved. Women will often turn pale immediately on seeing their lover and then get slightly red in the face as their sweetheart draws near. When two people who are romantically connected get within three or four feet of each other you will notice a very definite aura about them, almost an actual glow, and they will act as if they are in a cocoon together, as if they are more or less removed from the rest of the world. This is the effect of physical closeness upon two people who are in love.

But romantic kissing requires more than simple proximity. In addition it requires some degree of intimacy or privacy. This allows lovers to be themselves and to feel relaxed enough to kiss the way all lovers want to kiss. Even a public kiss requires some degree of privacy, which is why you'll see lovers stepping to the side of a busy street or moving to a spot on a sidewalk where they are shaded by an overhanging tree.

Some lovers can attain the romantic privacy they need by locking their minds together and securing for themselves a degree of psychological privacy. In this way they can kiss in public even in a crowded plaza and keep it romantic. But achieving that kind of romance in public takes practice and a certain degree of like-mindedness. At the outset, at least, you'll find it easier to kiss romantically in private.

Wilhelm Reich stressed how essential

this privacy is to lovers and he lashed out at society for making it difficult for young people to be together away from the prying eyes of their elders. But perhaps he underestimated the creativity of the young. If you put your mind to it, you'll find a place to kiss even if it means seeking out an empty stairwell, a shady spot under a tree, or the top car of a stopped Ferris wheel.

A nineteen-year-old from Hawaii had his most romantic kiss on a live volcano. He took his girlfriend out to the shelf where lava rolled into the ocean, shrieking with steam and heat every time a wave came in, now and then surging and making deep low explosions underground. Bathed in an eerie orange glow, they stood on the edge of land no more than two weeks old. It was three A.M. but hot enough to be noon in the summer. The young man turned to his girlfriend and said, "I really would take you to the ends of the earth for even a single kiss." For the next ten minutes they smooched by the light of the sheer power of nature melting rocks.

When I asked people to describe the most romantic places they ever kissed, their answers almost always referred to this type of ends-of-the-earth isolation. They mentioned an apple orchard, a beach, being in a glass elevator, out in a field looking at the stars, at a beaver pond in a secluded area, on top of the Eiffel Tower, or on a train ride together.

Those who enjoyed these kinds of romantic kisses often felt kissing was more intimate than sex. In fact when I asked "What do you think is more intimate, kissing or sex?" 50 percent of men and 75 percent of women said kissing.

What do you think is more intimate, kissing or sex?

WOMEN:
"I think that kissing is more intimate because I've found that if I'm having sex

with someone that I don't find too interesting personality-wise, then I don't want to kiss them at all. But if I'm romantically involved and really enjoy the person that I'm with, then I want to kiss them for hours."

"My boyfriend and I have been discussing this question ad nauseam lately and, frankly, I think kissing is much more intimate than having sex. Kissing is such a connection! I mean it's nearly impossible to kiss someone and not stay physically and mentally involved. Sometimes we surprise each other if we get more aroused and excited about each other by just kissing as opposed to having sex."

MEN:
"When we're talking about real good kissing, kissing is more intimate."

"Kissing, except if sex is damn good with a person I love."

Does kissing always have to lead to other sexual acts?

WOMEN:
"No, no, a thousand times *no!* Kissing in and of itself is wonderful and should not be taken for granted. My lover and I often sit for hours and kiss and touch and cuddle with each other without anything else happening and no clothes being removed (except shoes)."

"I love kissing for the sake of kissing. To me, kissing and sex are two very different and separate activities."

"Many men think kisses always should lead to intercourse, so I usually don't get *too* involved with kissing unless I want to end up making love."

"Kissing by itself can be very sensual and sexy and is not just part of a ritual before sex."

The opinions of these young women represent a bold new way of looking at the sensual aspects of kissing. They're suggesting that kissing can stand alone as a sensual pleasure that deserves to be enjoyed for itself without going on to other sex acts.

Kissing Tip

The following romantic things are often cited by men and women as getting them in the mood to kiss: taking a stroll through a park or along a quiet street, holding hands, romantic (not adult!) movies, music, intelligent open conversation, poetry, back rubs, fireworks, roses, dim lights, cuddling, physical closeness, candlelight, nice scenery, twilight. In addition, most men mentioned the smell of good perfume, kissable lips, a sexy outfit, looking at the opposite sex and getting turned on, and flirting.

Recent surveys indicate that people believe kissing is one of the most essential aspects of a relationship, yet men and women are increasingly reporting that there is not enough kissing in their love lives. For example, a recent survey of more than four thousand men showed that of all foreplay activities kissing was considered the most enjoyable. At the same time another survey indicated that many men want more kissing in their relationships. And many women rated the pleasure they received from kissing higher than the pleasure they received from any other type of sexual activity, yet they frequently complained that there wasn't enough kissing in their love lives. There is a growing interest on the part of men and women in kissing for the sake of kissing, all of which suggests that kissing is perhaps the most sensuous form of loveplay. Indeed, a lot of people like it so much they seem to think that they are somehow alone in their insatiable desire to kiss.

Many people told me confidently: "I like to kiss more than just about anybody!"

$\mathscr{K}$ISSABILITY

Stop and think of someone you'd like to kiss. What makes them so kissable? Survey results were nearly unanimous—good looks, a winning smile, a positive mental attitude, fresh breath, and beautiful lips and teeth. Not everyone is born looking like a supermodel but you don't need plastic surgery to improve your kissability. Just listen to what men and women say makes a person kissable.

Clothes and hairstyle

Women like men who wear fashionable clothes, and it's important to realize that fashions change. Bell-bottoms and a cravat just won't work these days, and I know because I've tried both. Study men's fashion magazines for ideas. Or ask a woman friend what looks good on you. Women are almost always flattered to help a guy select something sexy. Ask her, too, about a hairstyle that will work for you. You may hate it but if it draws women to you like flies to honey, how can you complain?

Men like women in solid tops, skirts, and the latest colors and styles. But the best thing to do is take the time to ask the guy you like what turns him on in clothes or hairstyles. Each man has his own special favorites. Some like a certain fabric, some a certain design, some a certain cut. Once you find out what turns him on, you'll be irresistible. Men are easy this way, much easier than women. One guy said every time he saw a woman wearing a plastic watchband he would want to marry her. Men are like fish, and the bait is hanging on all those racks in clothes stores. It'll even make him kiss better if he can see it or feel it while he's kissing. But you'll never know unless you ask.

Kissing compatibility

Many people ask me about compatibility with a kissing partner and I begin by telling them to forget horoscopes. Over ten thousand studies have proved them invalid. The true test of kissing compatibility is how well you get along when together. Do you enjoy each other's company or do you argue incessantly? Can you resolve conflicts or do they drag on? Can you enjoy a lengthy conversation or are you at a loss for words when together? Remember that sexual attraction may draw you to numerous people you are nonetheless psychologically incompatible with. Always ask yourself if this is someone you'd enjoy going on a cruise with if you weren't allowed to kiss or touch for the entire trip. Love is a journey and you want to make it with someone you're not only attracted to but whom you can talk to and enjoy day-to-day living with. These are the kinds of people you'll be most compatible with and the people you'll enjoy kissing most.

One final point, based on personality research. If you're a dominant type, look for someone who's easygoing and compliant because opposites do attract. Sure you may enjoy the company of other forceful personalities, but that's what's known as a narcissistic relationship—you love in them what's best in yourself. For a more interactive relationship and greater compatibility seek out a kissee who is the opposite of your personality type. Your kissing will last longer and be more fun and in the long run you'll enjoy their company more.

Fresh breath

When you're up close and personal you want your breath to be fresh. I once met a girl who insisted that her boyfriend brush before each kiss—with a new toothbrush! That's overdoing it, but brushing and flossing will definitely freshen your breath. So will drinking water because it flushes away bacteria. Mints and gum also work. Mouthwash lasts about an hour. Says one inventive fellow, "For early morning kisses, I have a small glass of mouthwash on the nightstand. Depends on how light a sleeper she is and on whether you can use the mouthwash without making it *sound* like you're using it." A tip for dining out is to eat the same dishes. And biting into an apple for dessert will also freshen your breath.

Lips

Pouty lips will attract people to you, but you don't need collagen injections to have sexy lips. Some girls say licking their lips keeps them shiny. Others brush their lips with a toothbrush to smooth them down. Still others have a favorite brand of lip gloss that works. But both sexes overwhelmingly consider a big smile sexy.

Lipstick

During kissing, most men (67 percent) don't mind if you wear lipstick. Twenty-five percent dislike it, usually because of the way it smells or feels. And 8 percent actually like it when you're wearing *flavored* lipstick. . . . Most women have a favorite color, but varying it might actually attract more men to you since some men are attracted to pink, others to red, and still others to beige, brown, or even ivory.

Stubble

Most women don't like kissing a guy with stubble. But 33 percent say it's a distinct turn-on. Try showing up for a date without shaving and ask if she likes kissing you like that. You might be pleasantly surprised. Fully 80 percent of women are drawn to the bad-boy type, so you'll excite her if you look like an unshaved thug. Said one thirty-three-year-old, "I love it when he doesn't shave for a day or two. He starts to look like a cowboy, and I just want to ride away with him."

When stubble becomes a mustache or beard, women are almost evenly divided on whether they like it. Slightly more (54 percent) say they like a clean-shaven face, while 40 percent admit to liking a mustache or beard at least occasionally. Says one woman, "Beards seem to make a man's lips more luscious. They feel nice when they're nuzzling your neck, too." And 10 percent say it doesn't really matter.

Looks

"What makes a person kissable is first and foremost their brain," says one woman. "You may be initially attracted to someone by physical appearance, but that usually wears off in about five minutes. I've met many people whose looks left something to be desired, but after talking with them for about half an hour, all I wanted to do was jump them. Long dark hair and intense eyes of any color don't hurt. And the taller the better."

You don't have to be a model to be kissable. While attractiveness might make people want to kiss you, it's more important to avoid being unattractive. Check yourself in the mirror before going out to make sure your appearance is acceptable. But when you're close enough to kiss don't worry if you're not beautiful. You're out of focus!

The $\mathcal{P}$HILOSOPHY
OF KISSING

I was gearing up to write a fifty-page es-
say on great philosophers and their kissing
practices, complete with details about the
kisses of Camus, Schopenhauer, Nietzsche,
and many more when I suddenly stopped
in my tracks and realized that what you
really want is a simple straightforward
explanation of how your philosophy of
kissing—yes, *your* philosophy of kissing—
can help you kiss better.

First of all let me demonstrate that you
do indeed have a philosophy of kissing.
Just ask yourself "Why do I kiss?" It's your
answer to that question which is your philosophy of kissing. The reason you kiss,
your motivation, the thoughts swirling
through your head when you kiss—all

this comprises your own unique philosophy of kissing. Whether you kiss to please
yourself, to please your partner, to express
your love or for any combination of these
or other reasons, your philosophy of kissing influences how you kiss and how
much enjoyment you get from kissing.
And it's those who stop to think about
kissing, as we're doing in this chapter,
who inevitably get more fun from it and
do it better.

Although you needn't study philosophy
per se to understand kissing, it's a remark-
able fact that the greatest philosophers
each in their own way identified crucial
ideas that can help you kiss more passionately. Let's take a look at three great thinkers to see how their ideas can help us kiss.

How to kiss like Kierkegaard

The Danish philosopher Søren Kierkegaard argued that whatever you do in life
you'll regret. In other words if you kiss

her you'll regret it and if you don't kiss her you'll regret it. That's the human condition because we can never be sure what is really best in any given situation.

How to apply this to kissing? Simply remember to embrace uncertainty when you're with your lover. Approach her and let yourself wonder, Is this the time to kiss or is this the time to refrain from kissing? Move closer, so close that you can feel the heat from her body on yours. Your nerves begin to scintillate with excitation, your knees get weak and at just that moment once again you'll think of Kierkegaard's analysis. To kiss or not to kiss. . . .

And when your lips finally do touch those of your beloved—for touch lips you will!—at that very moment you'll be inundated with a philosophical ecstasy that can double your kissing pleasure, for along with the enjoyment of the kiss you'll simultaneously experience the thrill of existential doubt about the rightness or wrongness of the kiss. Ah, what joy to doubt! What bliss not to know! Indeed it is doubt and uncertainty itself that excites our moral sense and makes a kiss extra enjoyable.

Whatever your age and experience level, you're human and to be human is to doubt. In fact I just heard from a fifteen-year-old who said she never knows whether to kiss when she's with that special fellow. I also heard from a forty-year-old who's always uncertain about whether to kiss her husband when he comes home from work. Two people so far apart in age yet so close in philosophy! Both enmeshed so fully in the human condition that doubt creeps into their most intimate kisses. The young girl also never knows when to break off from a kiss. The married woman says she can't tell if her husband is enjoying a kiss. Both of these doubting kissers know that no kiss has the perfect resolution, the perfect beginning, the perfect end. Theirs is a supremely human kiss, a kiss of doubt, a kiss of tentativeness. May all your kisses taste as sweet! For it is this very tentative quality that keeps young lovers on their toes and makes experienced lovers young again.

Do you ever feel uncertainty about a kiss? Why?

"Sometimes I feel uncertain because I think that I'm too quick to kiss or possibly lead people on by kissing them."

"Sometimes I feel uncertain because usually when I kiss I have feelings for the person but I don't know whether they have feelings for me."

"Sometimes I feel uncertain because I feel like I'm with the wrong person, like maybe I'm in love with someone else."

"Sometimes I feel uncertain because I think I shouldn't be doing this, he's too old, I don't like him, he dated my sister one year ago, or this is my friend's boyfriend, *What am I doing!* So clearly my body acts before my mind."

"Sometimes I feel uncertain because I wonder what the guy's real intentions are."

How to kiss like Sartre

Begin by dressing in black. You must obtain some French cigarettes, Galois if possible. And then you must haunt cafés wherever you live. When your lover appears look suspiciously at her. Imagine her in the arms of another man. Your pulse will race, your skin will get hot with anger, you will become infuriated and angry and you may feel the impulse to shout "Where is he!" But resist! Instead lean forward and kiss her. The jealousy seething under the surface will make your pulse pound and your kisses delightful. You're kissing the existential kiss par excellence and loving every moment of it. In fact you can't get enough of the kiss and you suddenly bound to your feet and take her by the hand and lead her into an alley and begin kissing her passionately.

While you are so occupied a waiter comes and pours more coffee into your cup. Five or six minutes later you return to your table flushed and excited, a new twinkle in your eye. People are talking about you. They are saying "Who are those two!" If only they knew! You are existential lovers.

Jean-Paul Sartre and his lover Simone de Beauvoir never married and they even allowed themselves to have other lovers. So whenever they kissed they felt not only a twinge of uncertainty but also a stab of jealousy.

You may be nervous about the existential kiss because you don't like the thought of another person with your lover. But you must conquer this fear.

The essence of existential kissing is not possession but respect for your partner's essential freedom. The point is to accept your own freedom and the freedom of your partner and to find an essential and necessary love with one person while at the same time tolerating that slight twinge of jealousy that can make your kisses doubly exciting.

Did you ever feel jealousy during a kiss?

MEN:
"I was kissing my girlfriend and we were kissing for a long time and I opened my eyes and I saw her looking around as if she was bored so I immediately started sucking on her lower lip and she liked it and she started to do it to me and, well, it kept her interested."

"If I'm kissing a girl and I think about one of her exes it's usually because she's having issues with that person and I just try to block it out. I don't want to think about them, I want to think about us. I don't like to feel jealous so I usually try not to think about it by blocking it out."

WOMEN:

"I was sitting on top of my boyfriend kissing his neck and then kissing his lips and all I could think was some other girl did this to him before, so I added a little bit to the kiss by biting his bottom lip and sucking on his bottom lip and then I started sucking his tongue and he loved it!"

"When me and my guy first started dating he had just gotten out of a relationship with another girl. I tried as hard as I could to get as much information about how she kissed him without making myself obvious about what I wanted to know. Then with every mistake she had made in mind, I corrected all those mistakes myself to the point where all he could think about was how perfect my kiss was compared to hers."

"I've been dating this person for two months already, and it happens to be that he's married, and I always try to kiss in a way that he can't forget so he won't want to go home and kiss his wife."

How to kiss like Hegel

The philosopher Hegel said that in every relationship there is a *thesis* and an *antithesis,* two opposing ideas which fight it out until they produce a *synthesis.*

Did I say synthesis? Look what's happening! While you and I have been talking philosophy, look who's under the linden tree. It's a guy and girl who were arguing a moment ago but who are now standing close together. It's Luke leaning over the upturned face of the lovely Greta and getting closer and closer to her, a light of anticipation in his eyes. It's Greta herself coming out of her confusion and despair with a sweet smile on her lips. And finally it's the lips of Luke floating down,

down, down, ever so gently, ever so softly, ever so much like silent autumn leaves falling from the sky itself. A rosy hue of excitation and contentment suffuses Greta's face as Luke bends down toward her. "And he kissed me out of the blue," she said, "and it changed everything." Well that's a synthesis for you. That's what a synthesis is meant to do. It's meant to make you feel different about everything.

The Hegelian kiss

Let's call the woman's thoughts and desires the thesis and the man's the antithesis. Of course there are differences between them. It goes without saying that those differences are what make the world go 'round. The thesis and antithesis are yin and yang, but Hegel takes yin and yang a step further by giving us the resulting synthesis. The synthesis is the feeling that comes about when the woman's lips meet the man's.

Once you understand how the dialectic works in kissing you start seeing that every kiss has the potential to change you in some way. Let me give a funny example. I recently got a distressing plea for help from a college student. "Why do you think my boyfriend doesn't want to spend as much time kissing as he does watching football?" she said. The girl's desire to kiss was the *thesis,* the boy's desire to watch the game the *antithesis.* They were in direct opposition on the issue of kissing.

"Every man has a weak spot for something erotic," I told her. "And if you can find out what this is you can often tease him into kissing you more. Maybe he'd like to kiss you when you're wearing a football shirt, who knows. The best way to find out is to ask him what turns him on then try out some of those suggestions in your own look or personality."

A week later she replied. "Thank you so much! My boyfriend got a scholarship to Penn State and he'll be going there next year and all he's ever cared about is football. So I took his jersey, tied it up really cute and surprised him Saturday evening (a big college football night) and he went absolutely nuts! We made out the entire game. I don't think he'll ever ignore me again."

How can you use the dialectic in your own romantic life? Just remember that each time two people get together they have the potential to become something better than they were individually. Seek a synthesis of the best in both of you. Celebrate that synthesis with a kiss and you'll be applying the dialectic in a way that would make Marx and Engels jealous.

And here we conclude our brief survey of philosophy, having seen that kissing can encompass doubt, uncertainty, and jealousy. We've also seen how it can lead to a new synthesis between lovers. When you consider these ideas and the ideas of other great thinkers you naturally expand your own philosophy of kissing, enhancing your capacity to enjoy a kiss and to give kissing pleasure to those you love. Perhaps that's what Socrates meant when he said, "No one kisses like a philosopher."

PART TWO

How
to Kiss

The FIRST KISS

I am going to die. I am going to die right here on the chaise lounge in your study, right here on this ancient couch that your uncle dusted off yesterday so that it would look good for your birthday party, right here in front of you unless I get to kiss you good-night. Oh God, I hope I don't have to die but if I do don't call me frustrated, don't call me hopeless, don't call me romantic to the extreme just call me desperate for this first kiss with you, hoping against hope that it occurs tonight because if it doesn't my world is likely to crumble like a sand castle and my life will never be the same.

Let's set the record straight on this important point. Every young lover is a voyager and the first kiss is the safe harbor toward which each captain steers his

vessel. Beyond all else it is the first kiss
that is the goal to be reached if love is to
ignite. Accomplish your first kiss and you
are Cortés staking your claim to the Az-
tec kingdom, you are Livingstone trium-
phant in the heart of darkness, you are
Romeo confessing to Juliet. It waits for
you, that first kiss, it waits upon the lips of
your beloved—soft, inviting, and chaste
as the wings of a dove.

Take for example the most romantic
first kiss in history. We are in the home of
a brilliant and beautiful sixteen-year-old
girl. She lives with her wealthy uncle, and
on this particular evening she is in her
uncle's library studying Latin. At her side
is her tutor, a handsome young philosopher who has a reputation as a gifted rhet-
orician. Logs are crackling on the fire and
this cozy couple is trying to concentrate
on the first declension but the girl's heart
is continually skipping a beat. For some
time now she has been wondering whether
her tutor regards her as anything more

than a mere pupil. The way he holds her gaze, the way his voice becomes soft when they're sitting together at the table, the way he follows her with his eyes whenever she moves—all this suggests to the impressionable young girl that perhaps he feels something more for her than simple friendliness.

And then her uncle comes into the room and says he must travel to town for a late-night meeting. Before the girl can reply her uncle is gone and she is alone with her tutor. Why does she feel dizzy all of a sudden? Why is her tutor smiling at her? Why doesn't she have the simple strength to hold the textbook in her hands? Why does her tutor slip into the chaise lounge beside her? Why does the book drop from her fingers? Why does her tutor lean forward? Why does her breath become short? Why does he gaze at her so? Why can't she speak? Why do his eyes look so alluring? Why is she near to fainting? Why is her tutor so handsome? Why does she suddenly want him to take her in his arms? Why does time seem to stand still? Why does he reach out for her? Why doesn't she run? Why does he lean closer and closer, so close now that she can feel the heat from his face? Why is her heart racing madly? Why does she part her lips ever so slightly? Why does she feel like she's on the brink of death? Why do his arms encircle her? Why does she want him to kiss her? Why is his face so near? Why does she lean closer to him as if to help him do what he shouldn't do? Why do his lips touch hers? Why do they feel so soft? Why are they committing this sin? Why does it feel so good? Why does she feel so happy? Why is she crying with joy? Why! Why! Why! Why! Why! Why! Why!

The first kiss between dashing Peter Abelard, the strikingly handsome and brilliant philosopher, and Héloïse, his student, took place nine hundred years ago and led to the greatest sex scandal of the twelfth century. Yet it has a lot to teach us even today.

Notice first of all that these were not just two people who met on a lazy evening at a school dance. They had a history together that spanned many months. Abelard was a famous teacher and he had sought a position in the uncle's house for the specific purpose of being near the girl he had fallen in love with—but hadn't yet kissed. Notice that the two were in a relationship that preceded their love affair. By the time they were ready for that fateful first kiss they had been flirting for months and they literally couldn't control themselves. Finally notice that they waited for the right time and place for their first kiss. They were discrete and secretive and most of all romantic.

You too can kiss like Abelard and Héloïse if you keep a few essential points in mind. First, develop a relationship with the object of your affection. Whether you're friends, coworkers, or members of the same sports team, your relationship will set the stage for all that follows. Second, engage in romantic flirtation with this sweetheart at every opportunity. If possible, let your flirtation continue for weeks, months, even longer! This flirtation will lay the foundation for the kisses to come and when you finally do kiss all those flirtatious days and nights will swirl around in your mind like a whirlwind of pretty leaves motivating you while your lips are actually touching. Third, find the right time and place for your first kiss, somewhere romantic and memorable, someplace the two of you can be alone together.

The story of Abelard and Héloïse may sound like fiction but it is perfectly true. The girl became pregnant, the boy secretly married her, and in a rage the girl's uncle hired thugs to attack him. The two were forced to live apart—he going into a monastery and she into a convent. But ever true to one another, they continued writing love letters and scandalizing Europe and the Church to their dying day. And to think, all that Sturm und Drang began with a first kiss that lit fires that could not be quenched.

Practice makes perfect

Should I or shouldn't I? Doubt, uncertainty, perplexity, confusion! Such are the anxieties that plague a first-time kisser, especially in the days and hours preceding a first kiss. These doubts can reach a feverish pitch until they become nearly unbearable and the poor lovesick initiate is almost willing to attempt that kiss just to be free from the torment of indecision clouding his days like a storm. But my advice will help you overcome your anxiety for I can assure you that preparation will get you through a first kiss—and preparation is 99 percent mental.

Although we're all born with the ability to pucker and pout, the art of kissing really develops and blossoms with rehearsal. This doesn't mean rehearsal with a director at your side. Instead, all you really need is mental preparation for the kisses you'd like to be doing with your sweetie. It's worth remembering that no lover in history ever succeeded at kissing without some rehearsal. Take Romeo for example. Long before his first kiss with Juliet he was rehearsing it in his mind. He was gazing at her and spying on her at a party in the house of the Capulets and he was dreaming about what it would be like to kiss her. Then when he finally got the opportunity he was able to kiss the way he imagined because he had prepared himself mentally. Peter Abelard tells us in his autobiography, *The Story of My Misfortunes,* that he was "utterly aflame with passion" for Héloïse and in that condition he was thinking of kissing the girl long before he got the opportunity to actually do it. Even Cleopatra was dreaming about her first kiss with Marc Antony, as the historian Plutarch tells us, and was planning his seduction carefully and artfully before their lips actually met. If these who are considered the greatest lovers in history planned and rehearsed their first kisses, shouldn't you? Make no mistake about it, this step cannot be overemphasized. Even the most fleeting mental rehearsal can do much to prepare you for a first kiss so that when you actually put your arms around your heartthrob your subconscious will take over and your reflexes will allow you to kiss with confidence and poise.

The key to rehearsal is to conjure up a vision of the specific person who is causing you sleepless nights and anxious days. Imagine kissing this paragon of beauty, wit, and charm. Imagine putting your arms around this incomparable model of perfection and moving your lips closer and closer. In your imagination I want you to see this cherub's eyes sparkling, I want you to feel the heat from her breath and I want you to taste the sweet nectar of her lips—not once, my friend, but many times! I want you to lean in, pucker up and meet lips with this vision of loveliness. Are you starting to get the picture? Are you running it through your mind and envisioning all the delightful details? Kiss and kiss again! Kiss in your mind and in your dreams for all you're worth! Because each practice kiss will prepare you for real kisses to come.

This is the kind of mental rehearsal that will ensure a successful first kiss. But important as mental rehearsal is, it's not enough. No, dear reader, to be a truly great kisser it behooves you to study the mistakes and learn from the successes of others who have crossed the divide separating those who have kissed from those who have not. I collected the following firsthand accounts in order to give you a sense of the wide spectrum of first kisses possible—as you'll see, they cover everything from the ridiculous to the sublime—

and from each you will deduce a little lesson in love that you can apply in your own campaign of seduction.

How is it, you ask, that lovers can remember their first romantic kiss so well that they are able to provide all these details? The answer is that most people can recall their first romantic kiss whether it happened ten or fifty years ago because it left an indelible impression on them. In fact 93 percent can remember their first romantic kiss and only 7 percent say it has unaccountably slipped from memory. Most people remember their first kiss because it was different, it was exciting or . . . because something went terribly wrong.

Do you remember your first kiss?

WOMEN:
"This is one of my favorite stories. I was very attracted to the boy involved, and we had been having shy flirtatious conversations for some time. One day we were

sitting together and talking and suddenly he looked me straight in the eye and said, 'May I give you a kiss?' After controlling my panic I squeaked, 'Yes, you may.' He then got up and got a bag of Hershey's kisses and gave me one! I blushed a lot, we both laughed, and he said he'd hoped I'd fall for that. Then after a few more shy looks he gave me the other kind of kiss."

"My first kiss with George was in my room. I was seventeen years old. We were listening to music and the moment was right. We leaned toward each other and I knew we were about to kiss. In anticipation I shut my eyes and puckered up, ready for my lips to meet his. They never did . . . he had his mouth *open* instead of puckered, so instead of meeting his lips I met his tonsils! When I suddenly felt this big wet mouth swallowing my face (no joke, he got my nose, my chin . . .), I burst into hysterical laughter. My first kiss started out so romantically and ended up with me curled up on the floor giggling!"

"Talk about stressful! The boy and I froze in place after discussing the inevitability of the kiss for half an hour. With that kind of buildup it was impossible to enjoy it."

"My heart exploded. I was one happy rubber-chested gal the next day. A New Year's party. I was fourteen or fifteen. His name was Gary, a boy my age, a schoolmate. My first experience drinking hard liquor (or any kind of liquor). I let him touch my breasts under my shirt. We kissed for hours on a couch in a den of a friend's house. Then he drove me to a place where we watched planes take off from the airport, soaring, blasting close overhead. More kissing. More thrill to the bone marrow. I still remember his breath and occasionally the scent comes back to me."

"I was twelve. He was a fourteen-year-old guy who was in a play with me in junior high. We had the two lead parts, and we fell in love. It was opening night of the play and we were waiting backstage. The play was a Western and I was a saloon girl, so I had bright lipstick on. One of the guys who used to flirt with me said, 'Madam, let me take that lipstick off your face,' then attempted to kiss me. Instead, Tom (my boyfriend-to-be) stepped in and said, 'No, let me do it.' He took me in his arms, leaned me back Hollywood style, and gave me a long, slow French kiss. I was thrilled and excited. The play went great! The next day I felt more mature and definitely happy."

"It was the last day of high school before Christmas vacation. My boyfriend and I used to walk down a seldom-used stairwell together, and on this particular day I was annoyed at him. While we were walking down the steps he said, 'What's wrong?' Instead of answering I stopped on the step lower than him, looked him dead in the eye, and planted one on him. It seemed to suspend us in time, and although I had never made love before I felt that this was my first time, too, especially since I became so excited I even had an orgasm."

MEN:
"I was fourteen years old and I kissed a girl I had a crush on named Karen. It felt great, though she was eight inches taller than I was. I felt like I was floating on a cloud. I was a little embarrassed because she kissed me in front of my whole soccer team."

"Surprising. Didn't see it coming. I was on a Ferris wheel at the time and wasn't sure if the funny feeling in my stomach was attraction or vertigo."

"My first kiss was incredible. I was fourteen and we were playing truth-or-dare at a party and someone dared me to French-kiss a girl that I and every other guy in my school wanted very badly. She was an extremely attractive girl with a fantastic mouth. I had no emotional connection with her, but the kiss was exciting and she also seemed to be pleased. That thrill will follow me for the rest of my days."

"*Fire, fire, fire!* Man it was wonderful! It melted me."

"A disaster. (What should I do with my tongue?)"

Overcoming shyness

Some people like to savor the shyness they experience during a first kiss. It gives them an all-choked-up-inside feeling and for them the initial shyness is what makes the first kiss so memorable. But excessive shyness can hinder your enjoyment. One way to reduce your first-kiss jitters is to try to have that first kiss in a fun or playful context. About 5 percent of people kissed for the first time during a kissing game. Kissing under mistletoe is a good example of using a nonthreatening situation to get things started.

Another way to avoid nervousness is not to ask for the kiss, which may lead into a protracted discussion. Remember the girl who said that she and her boyfriend spent half an hour talking all the fun out of the kiss? Asking may spoil the surprise and the wordlessness of the experience. On the other hand, many girls complain that guys are so attracted to them that they get kissed when they don't want it. To avoid this problem ask her quickly without getting into a long drawn-out discussion of the issue, or better yet tell her you'd like to kiss her, saying something as direct and to the point as "I want to kiss you." Then don't wait for a reply, just move in and kiss her unless she backs away or looks like she doesn't want it. Remember Shakespeare's line from

The Taming of the Shrew: "Kiss me, Kate!" You can start the ball rolling with the same line. Said one young woman, "One time I told a boy I was dating that if he didn't kiss me soon—we would *stop* dating."

Don't let inexperience stop you from having your first kiss. Remember that everyone has a first time. And they'll never know it's a first unless you tell. Try a gentle lip kiss if you're a guy. If you're a gal, do the same but keep your lips closed. If you open up you're inviting a tongue kiss, also known as a French kiss.

Try not to think about what can go wrong during a first kiss. For example some people worry about banging teeth! If something like that happens, laugh it off. Tell your partner you're so very keen to kiss him or her that you're getting dizzy just standing so close. Dizzy with excitement! They'll believe you. Then get back to kissing . . . and get dizzy for real.

What advice can you give a shy person?

"Shyness can be good in kissing, but you also have to know when to ask if you're doing something right. I'm a former shy person and I *know* this is difficult but if you're kissing the right person it should be okay. Not to mention everyone should have some degree of faith in their natural ability."

"Well, it's a pretty intimate thing to be doing. If you don't feel comfortable, start slowly. You don't have to initiate kisses if you're really shy about it, but if you get used to giving pecks hello and goodbye with your friends 'real' kissing seems to come more naturally."

"Try holding hands and nuzzling for a while, the kiss will come on eventually. Get physically comfortable with the other person first."

"Relax and enjoy. There's no correct way to kiss so don't worry about doing anything wrong."

"Let loose and don't worry about what you look like up close because usually the other person's eyes are closed."

How to begin

Do you realize that 90 percent of boys do *not* know when a girl wants to be kissed? They really don't have a clue. So it's a big help if you assist him in getting things started. Here's how—

The way to accomplish your first few kisses is to wait for a romantic time. Go out together and be sure to make a lot of eye contact. If your sweetheart is gazing into your eyes and smiling, this is a signal that the time is right. Move close and fix his collar or brush his hair. If he seems to like this contact, give a short lip kiss to test the waters. Another good first kiss is a good-night kiss. If accepted it can lead to more.

Most people feel they're putting their hearts on the line by making the first move. If you lean forward to kiss him and he leans back in shock, you may fear that you'll appear foolish. A first kiss is always a foray into romantic danger but you can minimize the risk by flirting with your date and getting a sense of how he's feeling. You can usually tell if a boy will be receptive to a kiss by the way he's acting. Is he smiling, looking into your eyes for a prolonged time, getting close and acting a little silly? These are signs that he's ready for a kiss.

How to get a boy to kiss you

If you want the boy to make the first move and kiss you, give him some hints. The best hints you can give a boy are simple flirting and getting close physically. Use any excuse at your disposal to get close. For example, if you have a portable radio you could tell him you want his opinion of a certain song and then put the headphones on the boy yourself. You should of course be wearing perfume, which will get his heart racing. How could any guy resist? Another trick is to touch the boy in some flirtatious way when you're close. Try brushing the hair out of his eyes, straightening his eyeglasses, adjusting the necklace he's wearing, or touching his arm when making a joke. Any method you use to get close and touch him will usually work. If you're both ready for the kiss and you get close enough it happens automatically. If the boy is not taking the hints, grab hold of his shirt and pull him right up to you and ask him what he thinks of your eyes or your perfume, drawing him closer and closer until your lips are within kissing distance. This is a surefire way to get even the shyest boy to make the first move but you've got to actually touch him by pulling him close for it to work.

If he pulls away and doesn't seem to like being so close then you're moving too fast and should back off and wait for another time—or another boy.

How to tell if a boy wants to kiss you

There are some signs you can use to determine whether a particular boy wants to kiss you. The most telling signal is how close he gets. If he can touch you with his elbow that's close! If you can feel the heat from his face on yours, that's close! Here's an offbeat example, sent in by a fifteen-year-old girl, which proves that simply getting close is often enough to lead to a first kiss. "The best kiss I ever had was with my friend Sean. We were on the floor next to his sister's bed at a slumber party while everyone was asleep. He hugged me and our faces were close and then he did something silly—he blew on my face like I was hot soup, and I laughed and blew back on him. Then he kissed me. I blew on him again and he kissed me again, and we played that little game for a while. In between me blowing on him and kissing he said, 'You just want another kiss don't you?'" The key to this girl's successful first kiss was getting close enough to allow the boy to do something silly and flirtatious like blowing on her face. Have you been getting close enough to the boy you're dying to kiss? You've got to get very close to him, physically close, or nothing will happen!

Another sure sign that a boy wants to kiss is when he gets romantic with you. Some boys get romantic in funny ways. They may just start saying silly things like "Gee, I'm feeling a trifle dizzy." You can bet that a boy who talks to you for a long time and looks at your lips and hair and face—a boy who's so fascinated with you that he can't keep his eyes off you—a boy like this usually wants to kiss you. And you can be certain that a boy who calls you a lot wants to kiss you because it shows he's interested. Ironically, boys who avoid calling you because they're shy may also be signaling that they're interested in you. Boys who try to make you laugh all the time are probably keen to kiss you because a boy will not keep telling jokes to a girl he doesn't like. Another sign that a boy wants to kiss you is when he acts nervous every time he's with you. When he's actually with you in person his nervous system is wracked by doubts and uncertainty and he can't help acting nervous. Take it as a compliment. And speaking of compliments, if a boy says nice things about you more than twice each time you see him that's another sign that he'd probably like to kiss you. The same goes for a boy who teases you because this indicates a playful friendly attitude.

Everything we've said about boys also applies to girls, with one important exception. Although girls may signal that they're in a romantic frame of mind, most of them prefer the boy to initiate the first kiss. Nearly 80 percent of girls like it when the boy makes the first move. After that, however, watch out! Once you're in a relationship, girls are just as likely to initiate a kiss.

How to get a girl interested

You've seen a girl that you like and you want to get to know her better. How do you begin? Smiling is the easiest way to break the ice. If you go to school together talk with her after class. Talking with a girl is the best way to flirt with her. Girls might even like talking more than guys do. You can sometimes attract a girl's interest just by talking with her for five or ten minutes. The best way to make a girl fall in love with you is to listen to her— the more you listen the more she'll like you. Girls have a lot to say and if you start to listen she'll like that and you'll become special to her. To get her to talk, simply ask her questions. Ask about anything she might be interested in. Asking girls for advice is a good way to begin. Once she sees that you're interested in the same things, you can take it from there.

The first kiss is a milestone for any young lover just as it was for Abelard and Héloïse. The best way to accomplish it is to develop a romantic relationship, find a nice location, and then get close and flirtatious and move in for the kiss. But even if you're an experienced lover whose first kiss took place many years ago, remember that there's always a first romantic kiss with . . . someone new.

The ℒIP KISS

There are so many different types of lips. There are rosebuds, red bows, full frontal smiles. There are Mary Pickford mouths with bee-stung lips. There are wide sensual lips that curve up ironically at the sides. There are lips that have a flirtatious little pout all the time—at rest, when talking, when smiling, even when frowning. (How do they manage that?) There are mouths that are small and dainty and diamond-shaped. There are thin, cruel mouths that scorn you and make you want to kiss them even more. There are mouths that have an especially full lower lip, which seem to be made for nothing *other* than kissing. It's no wonder kissing is so popular!

Without doubt, though, you'll find the loveliest mouths on girls blessed with genuine kiss-me pouts. Artists die for an opportunity to paint them, photographers vie for the chance to shoot them, boys hope they'll be lucky enough to kiss them at least once before they die. These lips are almost crying out to be kissed and the lip kiss is the kiss to begin kissing them with. The lip kiss is the most basic kiss and you do it by simply puckering up, moving close and pressing your lips to your lover's. But such a description is only the beginning of the story. Said one young woman: "I enjoy the *creativity* behind kissing—the many combinations possible using the lips." *The many combinations!* This is the key. And yet all you really need to know to get started is how to approach, what to do during the kiss, and how to break off.

How to approach

Imagine that your lover's lips are pressed together in a demure red bow. Try simply touching your closed lips to the lips of your lover. What passion such a simple initial encounter can generate! You hold back and remain lethargic, not opening your lips the slightest, simply touching them lightly to your lover's. That simple contact will be enough to excite you both to the core because you'll feel the blood beating in each other's lips.

Another approach is to move in carefully so that you make contact with only your lover's lower lip. As soon as you make contact, stop and simply settle into the kiss slowly and softly, savoring the warmth of your lover's flesh.

Initial lip contact can also be made rather haphazardly, slowly, almost hypnotically as the result of prolonged eye contact. After you've been talking with a lover for a long time, if you've been sitting close and looking into each other's eyes, you'll feel a tension mounting between you that almost draws the two of you together. Let this tension build and as your faces get close don't worry if your noses bump, simply tilt your head slightly and press onward until your lips touch.

As one young woman explained, "I have on impulse leaned over and kissed someone while they were talking to me sitting on a couch. They seemed pleased when I did, so I might try it again." A thirty-year-old fellow likes to hug his partner, nuzzling her cheek for a while. Then he goes for the lips. "But sometimes she isn't in the mood for lip kisses," he says, and if that's the case he kisses her cheek for a while.

What to do during the kiss

Unfortunately even in this revolutionary age some people are still skittish about kissing. Once they make lip contact they seem to be in a rush to break off. They may unconsciously think that lip contact is dirty or nasty or prohibited and these ideas may make them afraid of longer kisses. Such myths interfere with real enjoyment. You've got to learn to settle down, relax, and enjoy the lip kiss. "During a kiss I think about the feel of my partner's lips," said one woman. "I think about the positions of our bodies." Move your limbs into various comfortable positions to keep the kiss going.

What do you do with your lips and head during a kiss?

WOMAN:
"As far as my lips go, I tend to start slowly with some pressing kisses before going for the open-mouth thing. And I try *desperately* not to give fish kisses, you know, where it feels like the person is gasping for air rather than kissing you? I think people

with large mouths are more prone to that."

"I like *still* kissing sometimes, where we just hold our lips together without moving our heads."

"I relax and stay open to whatever might evolve. With some people a very soft feathery long peck feels right, with others more pressure and breaks seem right."

"My head really just moves my lips where I want them to be, but you can do many things with your lips like massage the other's, or suck on the other's, or just touch the other's."

How to break off

There comes a point during every kiss when you've had enough. Some people fear that they might insult their partner by breaking off, and as a result they let a worn-out kiss go on forever. If you're enjoying a really long kiss, all well and good. But when the time comes, you've got to know how to break off. Don't just rip your mouth away unless you want to alarm your lover. Slowly close your lips while they're still in contact with your partner, and pause. Notice whether your partner is initiating another kiss. If your partner is starting another kiss, then you must decide whether you still want to break off. If so, keep your lips closed and pull back gently.

How do you break off from a kiss?

"Either by talking briefly (I like conversation during such moments—something about noise deprivation, perhaps) or by slowing down to a beginning pace."

"Get off my toes, take a breath, move away from their lips to kiss somewhere else. My favorite technique is to break lip contact and rub noses Eskimo style."

"Close your mouth more and more and pull away."

"Slowly, lightly, so she doesn't know when I've stopped kissing her."

The $\mathcal{E}$ye kiss

So, exactly how does this eye kiss work? Let's take a bus ride to find out.

As soon as you get on the bus you notice a guy sitting across the aisle wearing a white T-shirt. Cute, unshaved, and young. He checks you out, his eyes holding yours for a moment, then he looks away. Next time his eyes meet yours he holds the gaze a little longer then he looks away again. *What's he doing?* Before you know it your eyes are lingering on each other for many seconds. The typical stranger will look away after a fraction of a second but this guy . . . *this guy is into you!* When he puts his eyes on you it feels like you just got pushed up against a wall and kissed.

Fortunately the eye kiss isn't reserved

for experienced lovers. Says a fifteen-year-old girl, "I do it all the time! It's hard to tell when I'm *not!*" In fact, teenagers usually experience eye kisses before actual lip contact. It typically happens in school when they meet the gaze of a classmate they like. Says a thirteen-year-old, "I saw the hottest guy ever and he gave me this little flirtatious look and I swear we were making out with our eyes!" Often eye contact will prompt a guy to introduce himself to you. Before you know it complete strangers are falling under your spell. You seem to have this disarming ability to draw people to you. And once you realize this, you're dying to try it out some more.

Eye kisses can happen anywhere, anytime. A seventeen-year-old says, "My brother and I are about the same age and he always brings home his friends and they're all cute. Well this one time he brought one of his good friends and I couldn't stop staring. After he left my brother smiled and said, 'You like him don't you.'"

Once you discover how easy it is to eye kiss, it's safe to say you'll be looking for opportunities to make romantic eye contact every chance you get.

Describe your favorite eye kiss.

MEN:
"It was a beautiful girl named Lindsay and I just gazed into her eyes and felt like I was floating."

"It was this girl I really like in school and she's my friend but she doesn't like me the same way."

"The last time I remember was with a woman at work. I felt a snap of electricity between us when I looked into her eyes. We'll see what happens!"

WOMEN:
"I've looked at many people flirtatiously but usually it's the guy I'm with or the guy I'm crushing on."

"Just so you know, thirteen-year-olds do this too. I did it with a crush. I just looked at him while we were slow dancing at a party."

"It was a complete stranger and I loved it!"

"I do this all the time. I'm always using my eyes to flirt with someone—to give them that sexy I-want-you look."

The TRIANGLE KISS

You're kissing your boyfriend, let's say, when you happen to open your eyes and notice that he's got a very sweet expression on his face. He's also got his eyes closed. You've been kissing his lips, but the way he looks with his lashes demurely down gives you ideas so that you begin to kiss him on his cheek at the side of the mouth and then little by little, giving him a series of rather quick kisses as you go, you begin to travel up the side of his face to his eyes, where you softly place the lightest, most tender kisses you can deliver, first on one eye and then on the other.

The technique here is to kiss from mouth to eye to eye and repeat, like a little isosceles triangle. *That's* why you learned geometry! For such an unusual kiss, a surprising 75 percent of women and 67 percent of men said they liked it. Because the triangle kiss has tender and romantic connotations, it occasionally appears in love stories. In chapter six of Hemingway's *A Farewell to Arms,* Frederic kisses his lover with some triangle kisses. First he gives her a regular kiss, almost to pave the way for the triangle kiss. Then when he sees that her eyes are shut he kisses both her shut eyes.

Tips for kissing the eyes

- Start with other kisses to lull your partner into a relaxed and receptive state.
- When your partner closes his or her eyes, kiss one shut eye gently, then the other.
- Return often to the lips to keep your partner satisfied. Think of eye kisses as a novelty, a diversion.
- If your partner is wearing contacts, be extra careful.

Do you wear glasses or did you ever kiss some-one who did? If so, what advice can you offer on how to kiss someone who wears glasses?

WOMEN:

"I don't wear glasses on a regular basis but for some reason I'm *insanely* attracted to men in specs. If someone wears glasses, usually they'll stop after the first minute of kissing to remove them because they get fogged up. Or it's always fun after the first couple of kisses to stop yourself, pull back a bit, take them off the person, and say something like, 'We don't want any-thing to get in the way, do we?'"

"I do wear glasses and experience has shown that two people wearing glasses cannot kiss unless at least one of them takes their glasses off. Better that both re-move them if you're planning on kissing for a longer time."

"I wear glasses. I usually have my con-tacts in, so it's not a problem, but I would suggest that you either take the glasses off—which can be sexy if the other person takes them off and looks or stares into your eyes—or just tilt your head more and be careful and conscious, or don't get so incredibly close to the person."

"I sometimes wear glasses. It's not much of a problem if only one person is wearing them. I say keep 'em on until they get in the way. No use taking 'em off before you ever get kissed . . . looks too desperate!"

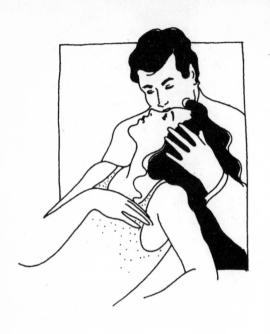

The TALKING KISS

O silent lovers, listen . . . people are talking . . . talking while kissing, that is. In fact 68 percent of your friends and neighbors are talking while kissing. How do they do it? "Not while actually applying both lips to her, but in between," says one man. Which is essentially the Chico Marx technique. When replying to his wife, who caught him kissing a chorus girl, Chico said, "I wasn't kissing her. I was *whispering* in her mouth." You don't have to say much. You don't have to keep a conversation going. You don't have to be logical or intellectual. Just whisper something romantic then get back to kissing. And whisper it right into her mouth!

What men say while kissing

"You're so cute!"

"You're the most amazing person in the world and the prettiest."

"Mmmm, baby!"

"I want you."

"I love you."

"You're beautiful."

What women say while kissing

"I'm liking this."

"It's okay. You can kiss me some more."

"Do you like what I'm doing?"

"Sometimes when I kiss I say 'I love you. How could I live without you? . . . Our moms should get together for coffee,' LOL, we really said that!"

What women want guys to say while kissing

"I never want to stop kissing you."

"I won't let anything happen to you."

"I like him to tell me all of his feelings for me."

"I like my partner to say he loves me and how beautiful I am and that he missed me."

"Once I was kissing a guy who thought it was fun to have a real conversation while we were kissing. I think it was about how our college basketball team was doing. It added such a fun aspect to the kiss that it made me want to do it again."

"I like guys to tell me jokes while we're French-kissing."

"I like my partner to say whatever he's feeling, whether it's dirty or sweet."

"Be my girl."

"Don't stop."

The $\mathcal{E}$AR KISS

Any man reading this chapter is holding gold in his hands and I'll tell you why. My survey revealed a number of surprising things but perhaps none as surprising as the difference between men and women when it comes to certain types of kisses. Granted a percentage of men do like being kissed on the ear and one has to admit that at the outset (in fact, the number of men claiming they like ear kisses is actually 12 percent) but a whopping 88 percent of women swear—some of them using effusive language like "Oh, God!" "Please, yes yes yes yes!"—that ear kisses are their favorites, or at least one of the kisses that excites them most. This unexpected difference between the sexes is good news for men because once you realize that your girlfriend probably likes ear kisses twice as much as you, well, you don't need any more advice, you can start kissing her ears and start watching her squirm in pleasure and giggle and get weak in the knees. Those are some of the reactions I have personally seen during the course of four hundred kissing shows at colleges and I'm not exaggerating or being metaphorical. These girls were literally turning pink with excitement, wriggling with joy, and otherwise reacting in the most silly manner simply because they were being kissed on the ear.

Now if you're a guy and you forget this you're doing both yourself and her a disservice because the statistics are on your side, so I recommend writing the words *ear kiss* on an index card and taking it on your next date. Frankly I admit I find it difficult to follow my own advice, especially when it comes to ear kisses because although they're fun they don't make me weak in the knees and they don't make me moan and sigh and as a result I forget to do them to her and in the heat of battle it never occurs to me that she'll like them. Quite honestly I often forget what pleases her best because I'm only human and I'm usually thinking about myself and what I like. Which is why you should do your best to recall this advice. If your partner is like the girls I've heard from and seen— girls who say things like, "Why *doesn't* he kiss me on the ears?" and "Can't you put it in your book how much I love ear kisses so that my boyfriend does it to me!"— well, if she's anything like these girls you're going to see fireworks and you'll be writing me thank-you notes. It might sound silly but it's true. The ear kiss is more exciting than most of the other kisses in this book. But don't take my word for it. Try it yourself and see.

Tips for ear kisses

- Kiss the ear as if it were a mouth. *Smack, smack, smmmmmmack!*
- Kiss the earlobe as if it were a lower lip—suck it and nibble on it, occasionally tugging on it with your lips and teeth.
- Gently insert your tongue into the ear. Trace the ridges and hollows with a light touch.
- Make little *mmmmmmmmmmmmmm* and *uhhhhhhhh* sounds. Heartfelt *oohs* and *aahs* are also a turn-on at this time.
- Breathe softly into your partner's ear. The sound of your breathing will be exciting. The tickle of your lips and of your warm breath will be a unique delight.
- But be extremely careful about the *volume* of the noises you make when speaking or breathing directly into someone's ear. The lowest whispers you utter are capable of being magnified into booming sounds that can startle or even hurt your lover.

- Whisper things to your partner. (Do you know why they call them sweet nothings? Because you can say *anything*. Literally anything.—"Honey, did you pay the rent?"—It's the feel of your lips and breath that tickles her, not *what* you say.) Try complimentary lines like "I love you" and "You're sexy" and even humorous quips such as "You have yummy ears" or "I wanna eat you up."

Do you like to be kissed on the ears? If so, how do you like to be kissed?

WOMEN:

"The ears are one of my favorite spots. If you haven't tried kissing your girlfriend's ears you're missing out BIG time. I think gentle is the key. Don't breathe directly into her ear because it's *loud!* and use your tongue lightly—don't just stick it in there—all you get is a wet willy. And don't forget about the area around the ear, the hairline, behind the ear (!!!) and the back of the neck . . . they're all connected."

"No! Stay away from my ears!"

"Yes, gently and dry. And not outdoors."

"Yes, as long as it's not too wet."

"I like it very much! I especially like to have my earlobe nibbled on and a tongue in the ear can be very sexy."

"Yes, but without tongue."

"Love it! Gentle but firm lips, a little bit of sucking and pulling, maybe the tongue slips inside, not too much saliva but damp is okay. I love to have my lobes sucked on."

MEN:
"Yes. So does my partner. Light nibbles interspersed with lavish lip work . . . *mmm.*

Sprinkle this with a few open-mouthed, hot-breath whispers, and va-voom. We're off!"

"Yes! Fantastic! Lick me behind my ears, under my earlobes, stick a tongue in my ear and I'll follow you home."

"Slight sucking of the earlobes does it more for me."

"Yes! I like my earlobes lightly nibbled and long tongue strokes on the outer edges."

"I love having my earlobes nibbled on and I especially like her to lick inside and put her tongue in my ear canal."

Kissing Tip

By watching and listening to how your partner reacts, you can learn a lot about exactly which parts of their ears they like kissed best.

The $\mathcal{N}$eck kiss

And you thought her *ears* were sensitive! You thought you had discovered something of real value in the previous chapter? You thought you had at last found the secret to kissing, a kiss to end all kisses, a technique that would reduce her to putty in your hands? Let me tell you right here at the start that while everything I said about ear kisses in the last chapter is true, nothing comes close to the kiss I'm going to describe in this chapter. And if you're a guy this is the most important chapter in the book because the most surprising thing the kissing survey revealed was that of all the places women like to be kissed their favorite spot, aside from the mouth, happens to be the neck.

Kissing a woman on the side of her neck and her ears speaks volumes about your creativity as a lover. A man who kisses a woman's neck is sharing a secret with her, a secret she may not even know about herself until you introduce her to it. When you kiss her neck you enter a world of intimacy with her that few women can resist.

After a few lip kisses try some feathery kisses on her cheek. She'll wonder where you're going. Almost immediately you'll get a sense of her delight as her body—not her mind—begins listening to you. Let your lips meander along the side of her neck and plant a few light kisses there. Notice her reaction. If she's like most girls she'll instinctively yield to you by becoming soft in your embrace. Continue in this fashion until your lips stray to the underside of her ear, combining ear and neck kisses for a double wallop that should quicken her pulse. You've made a smooth transition from mouth to cheek to neck and at this point you can experiment in whatever way suits your fancy.

Place tender kisses in the hollow of her neck, which is that small cuplike depression the chin touches when you tilt your head all the way forward. You could even lick that little cup as if drinking from it. Funnier still is to suck in your breath with a vacuuming noise while nuzzling your nose back and forth like a man slurping up whipped cream from a dish.

Then turn her around so you can see the back of her neck. By now she'll be pliant and cooperative in your hands and will follow your direction docilely so don't hesitate to take charge of her—gently, gently as you go. Brush aside her hair and exhale your warm breath onto the back of her neck, marking it for a kiss. Then bite her softly and kiss the spot. If she doesn't get weak in the knees you're not doing it right.

Most men know little to nothing about the power of the neck kiss because it doesn't excite them at all. In fact only 10 percent of men said they really liked being kissed on the neck, and none of them raved about it—"Drives me wild!" "Drives me crazy!" "Oh God, I can't breathe!"—the way women did. In stark contrast to this rather blasé reaction from men, 96 percent of women laughed, giggled, screamed, and almost jumped out of their seats when asked about the effect of a neck kiss. Men look over at them as if they're crazy. What's the big deal? they're wondering. The simple fact is that women like neck kisses about ten times more than guys. And no one knows why.

"I was fifteen when I had my first intense kissing encounter. I was sitting in the den with my boyfriend and I was getting very excited while he was kissing my neck. It was the first time I had had my neck kissed in this way. I was moaning quite loudly and getting very turned on and my boyfriend said, 'Are you all right?' Can you believe it! I had to stop and explain why I was so excited, which I found rather funny. Like he had no clue."

But when it comes right down to it, you don't need to know why a neck kiss is effective. All you need to know is the technique itself. May the following quotes give you both advice and inspiration.

Do you like being kissed on the neck? If so, what do you like most about it?

WOMEN:
"OOOOOOOOOO Yeeeeeeeeaaaaaaaa aaahhhhhhhh!!!!!!!! It gives me warm fuzzies all over . . . it really turns me on."

"You get chills or goose bumps all over your body."

"To have a man come up behind me, breathe on my neck, bite me and kiss me there is to send a thousand volts through my spine!"

"Oh Lord, I hate it. Just kidding! Along with my ears it's my favorite. I'm not quite sure what I like so much about it. It just feels amazing."

"Kissing, licking, or biting my neck is an incredible turn-on."

"I go crazy when someone kisses my neck. *That* is very sexually arousing to me."

"Drives me nuts!"

"Yes! My neck is super sensitive. I like the tickly passionate feel of someone's teeth nuzzling my neck, their little sucking movements, everything! I don't like

---

Kissing Tip

To avoid hickey marks on the neck, gently massage the neck with your tongue instead of biting or sucking it.

---

guys who bite hard or Hoover my neck. Good neck kisses don't leave hickeys."

MEN:
"Heck, yeah. Call it a throwback to caveman days, but there's something strangely intimate and trusting in letting someone lavish oral attention on your neck (noting that in the animal kingdom, that's the part you gotta protect from all attacks). It's soft, sensitive. . . ."

"Yes! It's like acknowledging that there is more to the body than just the face and lips."

"It's something pleasant, a sensation of being captured."

"There's a certain power that the kisser has in this position which makes me feel excited—a certain something about not being able to return the kiss (except perhaps in the person's hair) and having to store up one's erotic responses."

Do you ever kiss your partner on the neck? What technique do you use?

WOMEN:
"Yes, yes, YES!!! For lack of a better term, my current lover and I (he's not my boyfriend, kind of one of those in between types) are both neck fanatics (vampires, perhaps?). Kissing, using your tongue as you would on someone's ear, even nibbling and biting are good. Watch the biting though, some people don't like it and some bruise easier than others. An often overlooked place is the Adam's apple and right below, down to the collarbone and where the neck meets the shoulders. And do *not* forget the back of the neck—oh my!"

"A little biting can do wonders."

"Yes, firm kisses, a little bit of biting, trailing my tongue along their jugular or Adam's apple and along the jawline."

MEN:

"Little wet kisses up the throat to near the ears while holding the back of her head gently. On the back of the neck I like to stimulate the hairs around the hairline and on the spine. Electrifying!"

"I kiss her and slide my lips all over her neck, kissing along the way."

"Since I don't like to give hickeys (or receive them for that matter) I like to gnaw at a woman's neck by folding my lips over my teeth and sometimes using a little tongue action in between."

"If she's lying down on her back, I'll kiss and lick from her Adam's apple up to the underside of her chin, or else from the shoulder to ear (sideways sitting position) or after sweeping her hair away, the nape of her neck up and around to behind her ear."

The ESKIMO KISS

Congratulations, dear reader! You've accomplished the goal you set for yourself. You've kissed a sweetie a king himself would be proud to kiss, enjoying wonderful cheek kisses, lip kisses, and neck kisses with her. You've even used your tongue a few times. And now you're looking around, wondering what you can do next. Sure, like everyone else you've heard of the Eskimo kiss but you're not going to stoop to *that* silliness, are you? After all, that's for Eskimos or . . . for babies!

That's what I thought too until I stumbled across some research that showed what Eskimos *really* do. I thought it was just rubbing noses but was I ever surprised! And I'll wager you will be too once you see what's involved in an actual honest-to-goodness Eskimo kiss.

First let me explain that this kiss is popular not only throughout the Arctic but also among the Maoris of New Zealand, the Society and Sandwich Islanders, the Tongans, and most of the Malayan races (which is why it's alternately known as the Malay kiss). The technique I'm going to describe is also practiced in Africa and is the predominant form of kissing in Asia.

To begin, embrace your partner and bring your face close to hers. When your noses make contact, let them slide along each other. As the tip of your nose reaches her cheek, breathe in through your nose, savoring the fragrance of your lover. Lower your eyelids. Now comes the key part. With your faces touching, begin to smack your lips to the side of her cheek—without actually kissing! That's right, you're smacking your lips repeatedly, first on the left side then on the right side of her face. Smack smack smack smack smack smack smack smack smack smack smack. "What," you ask, "what in paradise is the purpose of this nonsense!" If you're anything like me the answer is going to surprise you. What you're doing with these little smack smack smack smack smack noises is you're making these smacking noises near her cheek while you're simultaneously *inhaling through your mouth* as you kiss the air—the air! you're kissing the air!—enjoying the delicious perfume of your lover. Now after you make those smack smack smack smack smack smack smack noises, your next step is to move your nose back and forth slightly, sliding it along the side of your lover's nose. Now and then bump the *tips* of your noses together. Smile and gaze into your lover's eyes while you do this. Occasionally bump the sides of your noses together as a variation on the sliding motion that predominates in the kiss.

And no, we're not finished yet! The

best is yet to come. There are a number of variations on the basic Eskimo kiss. Darwin described a Malay kiss in which the initiator of the kiss places his or her nose at right angles on the nose of the partner and then rubs it, the entire kiss lasting no longer than a handshake. Cook described a South Sea Islands variety as a brisk mutual rubbing with the end of the nose. Still others have described an Australian variety which consists merely of face rubbing. In many tribes the lover simply pushes his or her mouth and nose against the partner's cheek and then inhales.

Do you ever simply press your face into your lover's as a short interlude of rest between kisses?

"Yes, but not directly nose to nose—more of a nuzzling on the side of their face."

"Yes, usually I press my forehead against some part of their face."

Kissing Tip

Although many men and women consider it childish on an intellectual level, more than 95 percent of them occasionally like to rub noses while kissing.

Do you ever rub noses?

WOMEN:
"Yes, a little now and again."

"Yes, it's hard not to."

"Only with a child. It seems like a childish thing to do."

"I used to when I was a kid. We thought it was funny."

"I don't really care for it, but I've done it."

MEN:
"Definitely. Nose rubbing is loads of fun, alone or with smooches!"

"I like to *bump* noses."

"Rubbing noses works best when you simply want to hug her and keep your faces close."

The ELECTRIC KISS

What's wrong with me! I can't figure it out. Sometimes I feel I have no sense at all, I just follow the whims of the lady in my life as if I were a puppet even if the things she wants me to do are silly and frivolous. Take for example her latest diversion, the electric kiss. She discovered this one when she got out of her car last winter. Every time she touched the metal door she received a shock. So then she got the bright idea that instead of touching the door she would call me over and kiss me. Funny girl. She's always up for some lighthearted frolic and this discovery has killed nearly as much of our free time as her insistence that we take up kite-flying. At least the electric kiss can be done indoors so I don't have to go traipsing all over the country-side to experience it.

The kiss itself is rather easy to do, al-though it doesn't always work if you don't set it up right. The key is an environment where the air is dry because the buildup of static electricity is enhanced in low humid-ity. I have to confess that after she shocked me thirty or forty times I started trying to figure out ways that I could build up a static charge and surprise her back, but she's always one step ahead of me. Now she uses sweaters, rugs, blankets, curtains, whatever she can find, and she seems to have a strange affinity for static electricity because I'm usually on the receiving end of these shocks. I will readily admit, however, that if done in moderation and not taken to excess, the electric kiss can actually be fun.

How to get charged up

For an electric kiss to work at least one of the kissers must build up a charge. Now when I say build up a charge this is just scientific jargon for a process that no one really understands. (What exactly *is* a charge? Why is there a negative and a positive charge? Why should they attract? Nobody can explain this!) But we don't have to understand science in order to enjoy an electric kiss. All we have to know is how to get charged up.

I suggest you first turn off the lights. You'll see why in a moment. Now rub your feet back and forth on the rug. It's not necessary for your lover to do the same. When you rub your feet on a rug or take off a sweater or brush up against certain heavy drapery it is thought that you build up an excess of negative electric particles and become negatively charged—and when you're charged up with all this static electricity you'll give a shock to anyone you touch . . . or kiss.

Now slowly approach your partner but don't touch him with any part of your body because you'll dissipate the electrical field and sparks won't fly when you kiss. By now your lips are very close to his and in the dark you can barely see his face. Move in slowly. Part of the fun of the electric kiss is getting close and intimate without touching. It takes a bit of will-power and even a little practice.

As your lips close to within a fraction of an inch an electric spark will jump across the gap from your lips to his. *Zap!* If you're looking down at this precise moment you'll see a scintillating flash like miniature fireworks. You might even hear the faint crack and pop of static as the spark jumps from your puckered lips to his. Actual sparks of love! The surprise and shock of getting an electric kiss is often enough to cause young lovers to jump back in amazement. But you are a hardy soul and forge ahead. This is the time to lean forward and kiss him. For right now your lips are still tingling and there is no better relief from this tiny trauma than the sweet balm of a healing kiss. Ah!

Where to do electric kisses

One young woman said that she gave an electric kiss to her boyfriend after a party when they were standing in the hallway to go home. The air was dry and there was a rug on the floor. The conditions were perfect. The shock was so strong that the fellow jumped back and wanted to know whether she was hooked up to an electrical gadget of some kind. He was afraid to approach her until she explained how she did it. Then he wanted to try it himself. They stayed there for twenty minutes shocking each other with what seemed like lightning bolts from their lips. She said his mouth felt so tender and sweet as a result of the shocks that she was tingling with excitement for hours afterward. This incident suggests that the setting for the electric kiss must be just right. If you pick the location carefully, your experience will not only be shocking but also highly romantic as well.

The electric kiss will work in the following places, each of which has been rated by a master electrician in volts. Ratings from fifty-five to one thousand volts will give you a nice harmless shock, not enough to hurt you by any means. Ratings over one thousand volts can be slightly painful.

On a couch	55 volts
In a movie theater	66 volts
On a shaggy rug	625 volts
In a hotel lobby	800 volts
In a department store	75 to 1,000 volts
Under a wool blanket	250 to 4,000 volts

The BITING KISS

I act like I know everything in the world there is to know about kissing, don't I? Well, reader, I'm not as smart as I make myself out to be. And the proof of that lies in the stupid mistake I made recently when doing the biting kiss. You've all tried this, I'm sure, or if you haven't, you certainly should because it's a wonderful kiss. The biting kiss involves a little love nip, a gentle little bite into your girlfriend's ear or her lower lip. For years now I've been rhapsodizing on the pleasures of the biting kiss, explaining how exciting it is and how it will bring new zest and variety into your kissing sessions. Of course I always warn lovers not to overdo it, to bite gently, not to draw blood. But this time I didn't take my own advice. Not too long ago I was practicing this very kiss upon the ear of a little cherub who was giggling and enjoying it so much that I couldn't restrain myself, I just had to push the envelope further and see if I could get more of a reaction from her by biting even harder, and that's where I made my mistake. As I sank my teeth in for that last deep bite on her left ear she let out a yelp loud enough to wake the dead—this was around midnight— and then she ran to the mirror to inspect her ear, claiming I had drawn blood. I mean it when I say this is an exciting kiss, but more importantly I mean it when I say do it gently.

This kissing technique is more popular than you might imagine. In fact 78 percent of men and 84 percent of women like to bite—or to be bitten—while kissing. It might be appropriate to say that on some level we do biting kisses in order to express a little aggression, to dominate, to show power, to bare our fangs (so to speak) like a dog, a tiger, or a wild boar. The key word here is *a little* aggression. When you do a biting kiss you're not attempting to take a chunk out of your partner! Instead, you're demonstrating a little bit of aggression, certainly not enough to really hurt anyone.

When done properly, that is gently, the biting kiss is a great way to tease your lover, to make her sit up and take notice and to show your love in a new and unique way. If you're a girl a biting kiss is one of the most exciting kisses you can give a man. Perhaps because it gets through to him, it shows him you're passionate, and it's downright stimulating. It's a kiss of affection, of deep desire, of controlled aggression—with the accent on *controlled*. It shows that you could go further, you could be meaner, you could bite harder but that you're going to restrain yourself. And who doesn't love a lover who's got to restrain herself! It's a kiss every lover should master fully. Whether or not you like to do it, you should know how it's done just in case the urge comes upon you to bite—or to be bitten.

How to do a biting kiss

1. Gently nip your lover's flesh between your front teeth.
2. Tug up a fraction of an inch.
3. Release.
4. Then kiss the spot you bit.

Kissing Tip

You can vary the kiss by nipping the flesh between your lips only, so that your teeth don't directly touch your lover's skin.

The best areas to bite include the lower lip, the neck, the earlobe, the fleshy part of the arm, the fingers (especially the thumb), the toes and heel of the foot, and any other place you can find exposed skin. Use common sense as to when enough is enough. And be alert to your inner reactions. The biting kiss can arouse subtle aggressive feelings. Remember that love involves an element of aggression, and the biting kiss will let you get in contact with it in the most playful way. At the same time recipients of the kiss can get in touch with their feelings of surrender as they submit to your teasing love nips. These feelings are part of the normal give-and-take of any love relationship.

Do you like to bite or be bitten when kissing?

WOMEN:
"A little nip may be tolerable, but that's all."

"I like to be bitten gently on my neck."

"Yes, especially on my neck and ears. Wow!"

"Yes, both. I admit I do like to bite a

little. Not so much on the mouth but certainly on the neck."

"I like biting and being bitten when kissing, but it's got to be gentle."

MEN:
"My partner bites all over, including my tongue and lips. But I'm not too excited about it."

"I love my lower lip to be bitten when being kissed. I could playfully bite my partner for hours."

"Yes, if kissing other parts of the body besides the lips."

"A nibble or a tug here and there is nice. I like having my earlobes tugged at, or little half-bites around the collar."

Perhaps one final comment is in order here because a biting kiss can produce a little red or blue mark on the skin called a hickey. You can also produce hickeys by sucking the skin for a few seconds. Well, around eleven-thirty one night my phone rings and there's a guy on the line saying, "How can I get rid of a hickey?" I do a double take and say, "Did you have to wake me up to ask that question?" He says, "I just gave a hickey to someone I shouldn't have given it to." I explain to him that there's no way to get rid of a hickey. Doctors point out it's a bruise and like any bruise it needs time to heal. He says, "I heard vinegar works." I explain patiently that vinegar, cold spoons, pencil erasers—and any number of other home remedies—are all myths. Two hours later he calls back to say, "It's still there!" When it comes to hickeys, the best I can tell you is that a lot of girls cover them with makeup or a turtleneck shirt. But let me close with one final thought. Never be ashamed of your hickeys. Show them off proudly as badges of love.

The CANDY KISS

Who wouldn't be tempted to treat French kisses as invitations to go further with her! But for the moment resist the temptation and slow down. You'll discover a whole new world awaits you, a world of playful exploration in which anything can happen. And while you're searching around for ways to please her and amuse yourself you may be lucky enough to stumble upon a variation of the French kiss known as the candy kiss.

Perhaps you're sitting on a dock after a night of frolicking. She rests her head against your shoulder. You pop a mint into your mouth and look out over the water where the sun is going to rise. She stirs beside you and then kisses you on the lips. You kiss back, all the while keeping the mint hidden under your tongue. It suddenly occurs to you that it might tickle her fancy and give her a pleasant surprise to receive that mint during a kiss. Thinking along these lines, you slyly and carefully move the candy around until you can feel it there on the tip of your tongue, and next time she French-kisses you she encounters it, laughingly taking it into her mouth. It should come as no surprise that the experience of a candy kiss will linger long after the kiss is complete.

Never succumb to the temptation to think of a candy kiss as too silly or too unusual. Scoff at those who are too squeamish to enjoy it, though their number is legion. Poor souls! They suffer from a phobia of germs or were raised to fear such intimate pleasures. Remember it's a true classic. In fact it may be one of the oldest kisses of all. Indeed anthropologists speculate that when our ancestors transferred food from mother's mouth to baby's, the custom of kissing itself originated. Which means you'll experience a form of kissing that was practiced in prehistoric times when you play this little game. No wonder the feelings it can engender border on the infantile. What better way to get a girl to regress to a babyish level than to let her take candy from your lips!

Keep in mind that the candy kiss works best with mints, berries, and hard candies. It's a lot trickier with liquids. "We almost got thrown out of a restaurant once for trying this with iced tea," says a nineteen-year-old with a sense of humor. "He was attempting to squirt it into my mouth. We started laughing uncontrollably at the wrong moment, and that's when we had the accident."

Kissing Tip

Only about 20 percent of men and women have tried this kiss. If you can do it *and* enjoy it you deserve high marks as an advanced kisser.

Surprise is optional when doing a candy kiss. In fact sometimes it's better to set up the kiss by talking about the candy you're enjoying, discussing its taste with your lover until she becomes curious.

At last when you can no longer resist, when you have built up your attraction to an unprecedented new level, pass a candy from your mouth to hers. Says one enthusiastic fifteen-year-old girl, "On some dates we would pass candies back and forth for up to twenty minutes and it was a lot of fun."

Do you ever eat food or candy from your lover's mouth?

MEN:
"Once in Paris this girl came up to me and kissed me and she had a mouth full of champagne and she spit it into my mouth and that was really nice. It was the first time anything like that had ever happened to me. That was one of my most memorable kissing experiences."

"Any food (or other material) passing from mouth to mouth is generally nicer if it isn't too wet, so highly slobbered candy is a definite no-no in my book. Fruit (especially stone fruit such as peaches, apricots, etc.) tends to transfer rather nicely, as do cherries, dark chocolate, and various other goodies."

"We've held food between our lips or teeth to feed the other, to get that touching of lips that must occur when sharing food in this way."

WOMEN:

"I love to kiss while drinking wine. Tasting the wine on my lover's tongue is wonderful!"

"We've sipped wine and passed candies. Not food, though, that's a bit disgusting."

"We pass gum back and forth."

"I like to exchange hard candy during a kiss."

"Almost every night after dinner I put a chocolate mint on my lips and make my lover grab for it. We always get a laugh out of this."

"My lover likes to chew ice cubes, and he's fond of sharing them with me."

The SLIDING KISS

One survey response came from a fellow in his late twenties who said that when he was four years old his babysitter used to kiss him. She was a good friend of the family, almost like an aunt to him, and she babysat during the summer, usually wearing a sleeveless dress and watching television with him beside her. One day she asked him to kiss her and he started kissing her face and mouth, which she liked. "But she wanted me to kiss her so much," he recalls, "that I had to think of some way to do *new* kisses because constant mouth and cheek kisses used to bore me, so I started to *slide* my mouth down her arms. She was rather chubby and I enjoyed kissing the flesh of her arms. Then I'd slide my mouth all the way down to her hands and I'd kiss her fingers. She thought it was a great game. I called it the sliding kiss."

He may have invented this one when he was four but he's admittedly still at it. "I do the kiss with my girlfriend now and she likes it too."

So go ahead and *sliiiiiiiiiiide* all across her body. Treat her bare arms like corn on the cob and quickly rat-tat-tat a series of typewriter pecks along first one, then the other. Keep her guessing by constantly moving from spot to spot so that she has no time to get bored. And be as risqué as you want. Slide down her neck and shoulders. *Sliiiiiiiiiiide* down her legs too, stopping to put itsy-bitsy kisses on her teensy-weensy toes and then slipping and sliding across her back. *Mmmmmmm-mmm, smmmooooooooch!*

Subtle sliding kisses

Once you perfect the longer slides (for example, down an entire arm) you're ready for the small, subtle variations. During a routine lip kiss slowly slide your mouth from side to side. *What is this guy up to?* Take it nice and slow and savor your lover's mouth first from one angle, then from another.

The psychology of the sliding kiss

Some species, including horses and humans, regress to an earlier stage of development when making love, which is why lovers often call each other "baby." Knowing this fact can help you become a better sliding kisser. Don't think of kissing as a serious adult activity, instead think of it as a childish game. Study one-year-olds and you'll learn a lot about how oral a human can be. Were we *really* that way at one time in our development? More than that, on some deep level we're *still* that way, and when you get your lover to express this childish side you'll succeed in unleashing his or her fullest erotic potential. So go ahead and *sliiiiiiiiiiide!*

Places to slide-kiss

People like to be kissed in the darnedest places. Here are some suggestions from the survey. Slide to these spots and kiss:

- "I like to be kissed in the crook of the arm."
- "My shoulders!"
- "Between the fingers is nice. Toes too!"
- "I like being kissed directly in my armpit."

The WET KISS

Nearly everyone likes loud music when they're on a dance floor or at a concert but even die-hard partyers dislike it at three in the morning when they're trying to sleep. There is a time and a place for everything and that applies to wet kisses too. Over 90 percent of men and women report that they like wet kisses at least some of the time. But what is the right time for a wet kiss?

To answer this question I conducted a follow-up survey on the issue. It turns out that most people prefer dry initial kisses, then as things heat up they enjoy open-mouth kisses. During intimate kissing sessions the tolerance for wet kisses shoots up over the 90 percent mark. So start a kissing session with rather chaste, dry kisses. These are closed-mouth kisses. As things develop you can begin French kissing. Then at the height of a passionate encounter you can progress to deep intimate wet kisses.

Aristotle believed that moderation is a virtue and anything done to excess can be deleterious. His formulation of this idea is known as the Golden Mean. Between the extremes of insufficiency and excess lies the virtue of the proper amount. Not enough of something like saliva can be just as harmful as too much. You want to achieve a Golden Mean when kissing. Too much wetness and you'll drown your partner, not enough and she'll worry you're afraid of intimacy. Remember there is a time and a place for wet kisses, and that place is later rather than earlier in a kissing session. You may actually decide to wait until you've been making out ten or fifteen minutes before letting your kisses become wet.

Also keep in mind that different people

have different tolerances for a wet kiss. When such disparities exist there is only one solution and that is compromise. He must make his kisses drier while she must make hers more intimate. After some experimentation each may learn to enjoy the other's point of view.

If your kisses are too wet, swallow your own saliva. If they're too dry drink water just before and during kissing sessions.

Do you like both wet and dry kisses?

"I like dry initial kisses but wet kisses later. Affectionate kisses shouldn't be too wet. Sexual kisses are wet."

"I don't like slobbery wet kisses ever. But moist dewy kisses are great. So are dry soft lips."

"Dry is better. A little moist is great but soggy and wet is gross."

"Depends on the circumstance and the mood. Wet kisses are generally more passionate and reserved for the bedroom or other fairly intimate or intense moments."

The underwater kiss

The wettest kiss of all is an underwater kiss. These kisses can be done in a pool by submerging together and kissing under the surface. Many men are excited by the idea of a woman swimming underwater, her hair flowing gently and her body undulating like a mermaid. Such an archetypal fantasy may actually heighten a kiss. Women can use their understanding of male psychology to excite men by occasionally adopting the mermaid look.

To do the underwater kiss in a pool, begin by getting into shoulder-high water. Hold each other and take a deep breath. Commence kissing and slowly submerge a few inches below the surface. Don't interrupt your lip-lock. While kissing remember to enjoy not only your partner's lips and tongue but also the sensation of the watery cocoon all around you. Rise for air as needed then resubmerge. While underwater kiss gently to conserve air.

Kissing in a shower also qualifies as an underwater kiss and is very popular with both men and women. The same technique can be used on a summer day during a rainstorm. But don't try this in a thunderstorm. Your foolhardy narrator can attest to the fact that this is dangerous because he was actually struck by lightning while researching this book! Not an experience I hope ever to repeat.

Do you like to kiss underwater or in the ocean or pool or in the shower or bathtub?

WOMEN:
"Not underwater (yet . . . you've given me some ideas), but in a pool, yes. Chlorine is a little off-putting. Shower or bathtub yes, but not for long as it's too arousing and leads to other things very quickly."

"Yes . . . underwater—it makes me laugh, so it's more of a game."

"Kissing in the shower with the water rushing down mingles all the saliva and sweat together and makes things a lot smoother."

"Certainly in the shower. It can be very sweet with all that wet. Men seem to find this more thrilling, though, than I have."

"I like to shower with my lover and wash his hair and then lean against the cold wall in the shower and kiss one of those long slow kisses."

MEN:
"Whenever I was on a date at the beach we did it. It's shorter because it's only while you hold your breath."

"Taking a shower together and kissing sends shivers up my spine."

"In the shower we love to hold one another, kissing and caressing the other's body."

"I developed a technique that I call the Mermaid Interception Surprise Technique (MIST). This works well if you are too embarrassed to discuss underwater love with your partner. Encourage her to swim under the water. I personally find the sight of a woman swimming underwater to be supremely arousing, particularly if she has loose hair floating and swaying in the currents. Swim after her and make sure that your body is parallel to hers (usually horizontal) and you are facing each other. Reach out, embrace her and kiss, all while both of you are in a horizontal plane."

The Smacking Kiss

The sounds of kisses can be quite romantic and erotic. Such sounds are usually unintentionally produced when puckered lips pull apart with a slight inhalation or *smmmmmmmack*. Upon hearing this noise lovers tend to giggle or actually start laughing. Not infrequently the mirth produced by a smacking kiss will lead a boy to giggle so much he'll double up with surprised merriment and break apart and have to stop kissing for a moment. Often the sound of his laughter will cause his girlfriend to start giggling too and any further kisses between them will become impossible for a span of some minutes while each tries to settle down and get serious about kissing.

Another common but unfortunate reaction to the smacking kiss is embarrassment. Usually this is the result of a feeling of self-consciousness that overwhelms a sensitive soul upon hearing his kiss. Bashful lovers worry that they are producing altogether too much noise. The best remedy for embarrassment is to laugh it off and continue kissing. If necessary, try kissing silently. Alternately you could make a joke and intentionally overdo the sound of your next kiss.

For the majority of people, however, kissing sounds are fun to occasionally hear because they intensify the experience. Three out of four people surveyed enjoyed the sounds of kisses and considered them erotic and stimulating. One person in five also liked making little *oohs* and *aahs* and hearing their partner involuntarily moan now and then. And while most people prefer a natural kissing sound, a few prefer more exaggerated noises. You can easily vary your style until you and your partner find the sounds you enjoy best.

Do you like the noise kisses make?

WOMEN:
"I love the sounds of the mouth, teeth, tongue, and saliva and also the noises emitted from us from being excited. They increase the intensity I bring into the kissing."

"I like the sounds of kissing together with silence or nature in the background: the wind, birds, distant traffic, children playing, etc."

"If we're alone the answer is a big YES—it's a turn-on."

"Yes if they're incidental and not intentionally exaggerated."

"Yes, I love it. The noise is a great turn-on."

"I like the noise if it's *me* making it—I don't like listening to other couples."

$\mathcal{L}$IP-O-SUCTION

I learned about this kiss from a group of young college students. One of them drew a picture on the back of her vocabulary test when I was teaching a summer class at Boston College and she brought it up to me. In the drawing the man kissed the upper lip while the woman simultaneously kissed the lower lip. "It's called lip-o-suction," she said, laughing while her girlfriends gathered around, and she started explaining it to me. "You suck in the lip when you kiss and you suck it in a pulsating action like this." She held up her hands and started rhythmically grasping the fingers of one hand with the fingers of the other. Her friends were laughing and nodding in agreement.

Naturally I began researching it that very afternoon and what I found out convinced me that lip-o-suction is one of the most important kisses in the book. But I discovered to my amusement that lip-o-suction is actually thousands of years old. The *Kama Sutra* says it's accomplished when a man kisses the upper lip of a woman while she in return kisses his lower lip. Then they reverse. The modern version adds a *sucking* action to the kiss, a highly sensual element that gets the lovers intimately involved with each other's mouths.

Says a twenty-five-year-old woman, "It's a brand new kiss in America, popular because it's something new and requires the use of the lips instead of just the tongue." A thirty-four-year-old says she thinks the kiss is becoming more popular "because people have seen it in movies and on TV recently." Since discovering the kiss I've heard from countless high school and college students who do it all the time.

How to do lip-o-suction

1. The boy kisses the girl's upper lip.
2. She simultaneously kisses his lower lip.
3. Then they reverse. He kisses her lower lip while she kisses his upper lip.
4. The person kissing the lower lip occasionally sucks and bites it.
5. The sucking and biting is done in a pulsating action—kiss kiss kiss kiss. This rhythmic action gives lip-o-suction a unique feel.

What is your experience with lip-o-suction?

"We started kissing very softly and slowly and at the same time with passion and I took his lip into my mouth and sucked on it and then bit it. He looked at me like I had performed some miracle and I knew he liked what I was doing."

"When doing this for the first time you should be gentle and not aggressive. Try to gently caress your partner's lip with your two lips."

"Try to make sure you keep the suction going between you and your partner for at least five seconds at a time."

"It's a fun way to get to know one another, and you'll learn if he's interested in you or not. The way your partner does lip-o-suction tells you a lot about the person."

Kissing Tip

Try sucking in the lip to a set rhythm, such as every two or three seconds for a hypnotic, sensual effect. As a twenty-year-old student described it, "I like sucking her lower lip in short pulses in between my lips, and it's really a turn-on when she sucks back at the same time on my upper lip."

Standing in a doorway after a wonderful evening together you decide to kiss your

boyfriend good-night. You begin inno-
cently enough with a regular kiss but suddenly your mouth slips down until you're
locked onto his lower lip while he sucks
your upper lip. You draw him in actively,
pulling his lower lip deep into your
mouth. It tastes like an apricot—only it's
softer! Meanwhile you can feel him passionately swallowing your upper lip. So
that's the way he wants to kiss! Well, two
can play at this game. Now it's a little tug-
of-war between you, a brief wrestling
with the lips. You never knew he was so
insistent! He never realized you were so
wild and uninhibited! Your heart is racing, your lips are throbbing, and you can't
tell where your face ends and his begins.

Before long you each feel that strange
erotic presence that seems to hover over
lovers in the midst of lovemaking like the
fluttering of the wings of birds. A thousand impulsive thoughts rush through
your mind. How long will the kiss last?
What if you lose control? Will your lips

stretch permanently out of shape? What does it mean now that you've kissed this way—so close, so sensually? What's he thinking? Will he consider you a loose and immoral woman? But he's sucking your upper lip like a madman himself!

Then mercifully a blissful feeling rises from your toes and melts through your blood so that you're not thinking, you're simply kissing more passionately than ever. And you don't even care if you lose control. Your eyes close as his lip-o-suctioning continues. You relax into the kiss, now letting him take the lead, now reasserting control yourself.

Lip-o-suction. It may sound funny. It may even feel funny. It will certainly do funny things to you.

The *T*EASING KISS

After a while kissing can get too serious and even the most staid and stuffy lover will tell you there comes a time when you need to do something out of the ordinary to reduce the monotony that creeps into a repeated activity. The teasing kiss is a kisser's kiss, the one to turn to when all other kisses have been kissed, when your lips feel like cardboard and your tongue is tired and dry, when you're about to throw your hands up in despair and scream: "Kissing isn't all it's cracked up to be!" The teasing kiss introduces something out of the ordinary into overly serious necking.

How to do the teasing kiss

1. Begin by kissing a few times so that you establish a rhythm of kisses to the point where your partner expects another one.
2. Break lip contact and wait for your partner to lean toward you for the next kiss.
3. Timing is important here. As your partner leans forward you lean forward also *but don't allow your lips to touch.* The purpose of leaning forward is to draw him onward and mislead him into thinking that another kiss is imminent.
4. Just before your mouths meet lean back quickly and just far enough so that he can't reach you with a kiss.
5. If he smiles and gets feisty you know you've done it right.

Some people misinterpreted the whole idea of the teasing kiss. Said one woman, "No, I don't like to be teased therefore I don't do it to others, that's mean." Certainly a real tease can be mean, but playful teasing is a part of lovemaking. And some men, trapped in a role they think is masculine, can't let themselves be playful. One young man from Spain said, "No, I don't tease because it's too typically feminine."

Kissing Tip

A variation of the tease is the pause, where you wait a second or two before returning your partner's kiss. Watch their eyebrows go up in frustration as you withhold the expected return kiss.

Do you ever tease your partner with a kiss?

WOMEN:
"Guilty as charged."

"Sometimes I wait before returning a kiss. It's fun to play cat and mouse."

"Yes. He can be teased by my kissing his mouth and pulling away before he fully responds."

"I've teased and this can be very erotic. Once a man held me back from kissing him—he would kiss me and then wait quite a while before kissing me again. He prolonged our pleasure that way, hovering over me and sensing my excitement."

MEN:
"I get close enough and then pull back before the kiss is given to make my partner want to give it even more."

"The most simple form of torture is where you *don't* do something that she wants, but you're really close and you could kiss her yet you tease her mercilessly."

"I use the tease technique because it's exquisitely excruciating. The longer you hold out the more enthusiastic the eventual 'catch!'"

The statue kiss

The statue kiss, a popular variation of the teasing kiss, starts when your girlfriend says, "Honey, let's play a game."

You smile at her and wonder what she has in mind.

"Stand still and don't move for one minute," she says. Intrigued, you stand frozen as she has instructed. "Now, honey," she continues, "I'm going to kiss you for a minute and you have to stand still and not kiss me back. Okay?"

Smiling and thinking this is going to be child's play, you nod. "Of course, dear, whatever pleases you. Go ahead and kiss away to your heart's content. You can kiss for as long as you wish and I won't move a muscle."

And so she begins. First she rubs her body against yours. This is an unexpected turn of events! You long to put your arms around her and pull her to you. But you promised to be still. Now she hugs you and begins to kiss you. How can you remain motionless! But you promised to take it like a man. You must yield to her and receive her kisses no matter how tempting it might be to return them.

"My boyfriend never got so excited as when I told him he couldn't kiss me back for one full minute," says a girl who is a big advocate of the statue kiss. "He wasn't allowed to move although the only thing preventing him from moving was his own willpower."

If your boyfriend has a hard time understanding the rules, ask him whether he's ever played freeze tag (also known as statue tag, a game in which tagged players must remain motionless). Challenge him to stand at attention as if you were his drill sergeant.

Changing how someone kisses you

Eight out of ten people have occasionally had a partner who kissed in a style they didn't like. "I love my boyfriend," says one girl, "I just don't like the way he kisses. How can I change him?" The answer I gave her is that you can use a statue kiss. You tell him you're going to show him *how* you like to be kissed for one full minute while he has to stand there and take it.

One of the unexpected by-products of this kiss is that you learn how your partner likes to be touched and kissed. Notice how your girlfriend is teasing you and playing with you, how she runs her hands up and down your chest, how she presses her lips to yours, whether she uses her tongue, and anything else she does. This is a good indication of how *she* would like to be kissed. When the minute is up and the game is over, tell her she has to stand still and take it from *you*.

"I've told my boyfriend sometimes not to move while I kiss him. If he tries to respond while I'm kissing him, I tell him to be still—just to feel. This usually makes him very excited."

"You know what's really fun? When you kiss a guy and you tell him not to kiss you back so that you're doing everything, guiding the entire kiss. It's such a sexy thing to do!"

The
Butterfly Kiss

"And we're there on the couch side-by-side and she's got her face up next to mine and I'm feeling really peaceful and drowsy when out of nowhere comes this fluttering sensation like a butterfly's wings brushing up against my cheek, this infernal tickling sensation that sends a sort of vibration through me. If I didn't know better I would have thought a soft puppy was in her place or a feather or the petals of a flower trembling on the breeze. So I look down at her and do you know what she was doing? She was sort of laying there with her cheek touching mine and she was simply batting her eyelashes at me like she was flirting with me, only her eyelashes were so close they were touching my cheek and brushing up and down and making me feel so funny all over I just wanted to hold her in my arms and squeeze her and never let her go. 'What are you doing?' I said. She looked up at me and said, 'It's a butterfly kiss, Charlie, and it means I love you.' I'll never forget it."

Without doubt the butterfly kiss can make any intimate kissing session memorable. It's also easy to do.

How to do a butterfly kiss

1. Put your face close to your partner's cheek.
2. Flutter your eyelashes against your partner's cheek by slowly opening and closing your eyes.
3. Vary the kiss by fluttering your eyelashes slowly against your partner's neck or eyelashes.
4. Remember to do it slowly and make sure your eyelashes are touching your lover's face. If it's quiet you can actually hear the

sound of the eyelashes brushing against the skin.

Do you ever give your lover a butterfly kiss? What advice can you offer for those trying it for the first time?

WOMEN:
"Usually it's in conjunction with sleeping with them, sort of a sexual afterglow activity because it requires the person to be relaxed and still for a while. It's very delicate. Be relaxed and wait for a quiet time to try it."

"I like brushing my eyelashes against his neck. It helps if you laugh while doing it."

"I think people have liked it because I have long eyelashes. Still, it seems men need more direct touching than that, so a butterfly kiss may be a good wake-up technique. Get really close and blink as fast as you can."

MEN:

"I usually do this when I'm in a playful mood. Don't get too close to the face. Stay far enough away so that the eyelashes just touch."

"This is a nice snugly kiss for me when I'm in a romantic mood rather than an all-out sexual mood. It's a friendly way of showing affection and being close to my partner without being too vigorous. My only advice is to make sure the recipient stays relatively still so as not to poke any body parts (e.g., ears, nose, etc.) into the eye of the kisser."

"It's fun and always brings a giggle."

"It feels bizarre if you push your right/left cheeks together, getting literally eye-to-eye and blinking at each other. I discovered this kiss on my own. As far as advice? Hmm. Well, *necks* are rather receptive, too. And *belly buttons,* but this might go beyond your definition of *kiss*."

Kissing Tip

Keep in mind that 75 percent of men and 40 percent of women have never experienced a butterfly kiss. So you can often give your lover a pleasant *surprise* with this one.

The LONG KISS

Once upon a time there was a beautiful princess who vowed that she would marry only if a man's kiss convinced her that he was the perfect match. Hearing this the king issued a royal proclamation stating that he would give his daughter in marriage to the first man whose kiss was extraordinary enough to make the young woman faint with pleasure. But he added that all who failed to please her would be put to death.

The princess was so beautiful that men from near and far flocked to the palace to try to win her even at the risk of their lives. Upon arrival each contestant was led into a small antechamber where the princess reclined upon a plush velvet love seat. The would-be suitor was allowed to kiss the princess in any way he wished. The first man bent at the waist and kissed her forehead but she complained he was too timid. The second man kissed her hand but she complained he was too formal. The next man kissed her foot but she laughed and said he was too ridiculous. Another man immediately put his tongue into her mouth in hopes of exciting her but she began to gag. The king had each of these unfortunates beheaded.

In desperation the royal family sent a messenger to the far reaches of the kingdom seeking men with new types of kisses. Next morning an ugly old gnome was first in line. When he entered the kissing chamber the princess nearly swooned with horror and sat back on her couch thinking that no matter what his kiss was like she would reject him.

The gnome, who hardly even looked human, staggered forward and began kissing her. His kiss lasted such a long time that the princess started to feel dizzy. An attendant consulting a chronometer was amazed to see the minutes pass . . . one . . . two . . . three . . . and still the kiss continued. Meanwhile the princess was wishing the deformed dwarf would stop because she was breathless and her head was swimming and she felt a strange tension in her nerves. And yet the kiss continued . . . four . . . five . . . six minutes. At this point something strange happened to the young woman—she suddenly felt that she had come up for air from underwater and could breathe again. Yet she was still lip-locked with the gnome and in fact he was kissing her more insistently than ever. The kiss seemed to last for hours and eventually the girl's senses grew numb and all she felt was a burning in her blood like a slow fire. True, she could hear the voices of other contestants outside the antechamber but she made no move to stop the kiss for something had begun to warm her heart. Before long she found herself kissing back passionately. More minutes flew by until finally without warning the princess dropped onto the love seat in a dead faint.

Quickly the old man stepped aside and covered his face with his hood. The attendant rang a bell and instantly the door burst open and six or seven dukes pushed their way into the small chamber.

There was an exclamation of chagrin from the crowd when they saw that the princess had fainted but before anyone could lift a hand to assist her she fluttered her eyelids and sat up. To everyone's amazement she smiled.

One of the princes whirled toward the gnome.

"You've been in here all morning!"

Unperturbed the small figure replied, "Now ask the princess for her answer."

The young woman was surprised for

something in her heart prompted her to speak and without thinking she heard herself saying, "He is the one."

There was a murmur of dismay.

"He is the one I will marry."

The crowd stood back in shock, but at this the gnome threw off his hood and was miraculously transformed into a charming young prince. All the dukes gasped in wonder. Tears of happiness welled up in the princess's eyes, and true to her word she married him the next day in a magnificent royal ceremony. Naturally they lived happily ever after.

How to perfect the long kiss in six easy steps

1. Kiss your lover squarely on the lips. You must begin with the basics and a good solid lip kiss is the foundation of any long kiss.
2. Hold the kiss tightly so that your lips are in contact all around. This ensures that

you have a good seal on each other's mouths.

3. Prolong the kiss until you feel somewhat breathless. Part of the fun of the long kiss arises from the slight feeling of breathlessness that occurs while doing it.

4. Without breaking lip contact begin to breathe through your nose. This is the trickiest step. If you find it impossible to breathe through your nose you'll have to break off from the kiss and start at the beginning.

5. During the kiss don't forget to listen for the sound of your lover's breathing. This is another joy of the long kiss. Since the two of you are breathing through your noses you'll usually become aware of each other's breathing patterns and as a result you'll feel even closer.

6. Swallow when necessary but don't break lip contact. In this way you can prolong a kiss for many minutes without interruption.

Dos and don'ts of the long kiss

Do:

- Snuggle and cuddle during the long kiss.
- Be passive at times and merely keep your lips in contact with your lover's. In other words simply stand together with your lips touching while you make the tiniest little kissing actions with your mouth. Not much more needs to be done at this point for the long kiss to work its magic. The simple fact that the kiss is continuing for so many minutes will send keen shocks through your nerves and body.
- Get used to kissing for extended periods of time. This kiss offers a unique opportunity for uninterrupted mouth-to-mouth contact with your lover.
- Combine the long kiss with the French kiss and other types of kisses. One of the benefits of mastering the long kiss is that it can be combined with virtually every other

kiss. And by combining the long kiss with other kisses you can prolong your favorite kisses indefinitely.

- Stand or sit close to your partner during the long kiss to convey a feeling of love and connection.

Don't:

- Don't panic. Some people get anxious during a long kiss because they feel they're suffocating. Just remember to breathe through your nose and you'll be fine.
- Don't hyperventilate. Some novices get so excited when doing long kisses that they begin to breathe too rapidly. This can make you dizzy. Relax and enjoy the long kiss by breathing normally through your nose.
- Don't gasp for air when you break lip contact. Not only is this bad manners but it will make people think you can't tolerate long kisses. Instead smile and give your lover a knowing nod as if to say, "I can't wait to do that again."

According to *The Guinness Book of World Records* the longest continuous kiss under strict rules allowing no breaks occurred in 2001 in New York City and lasted thirty hours and fifty-nine minutes. Let that be an inspiration to you! Although you needn't set a world record, keep in mind that longer kisses are generally more erotic than shorter ones. Your lover will be delighted when he finds that what he expected to be a short kiss turns out to be a long, deep one instead. And if you can kiss for four or five minutes straight you're doing better than 98 percent of your friends and neighbors. Most people kiss for no more than sixty seconds before breaking lip contact.

How long do your longest kisses last?

MEN:
"When it's quite dark and cool, when we're close and drowning in love, well . . . a few minutes at least. Warm breath—by

nose or otherwise—is an aspect of long
kisses I could definitely get used to."

"About forty-five to sixty seconds.
Usually seven to ten seconds."

"I guess it could go for a minute, one
nice long kiss."

"A couple of minutes."

"Three minutes."

WOMEN:
"Until I run out of breath."

"My longest kiss lasted about one-half
to three-quarters of an hour. That was
with my first boyfriend. I like kisses over
one minute long."

"Maybe a minute?—as long as I can
breathe and there's some variation. Actually I'd probably prefer running a lot of
kisses together."

"My longest kisses last four to five

minutes. I love long kisses! The length of a kiss depends on the type of kiss and our moods. The kisses range from pecks (one second) to French kisses (four to five minutes). I tend to do more French kissing and these are longer-lasting for me than closed-mouth kisses. I'd say the average length of a kiss is twenty-five seconds."

"Usually two or three minutes per kiss. I like them to last as long as possible."

Long kissing sessions

In addition to long kisses many people love long kissing sessions. Also known as necking sessions or simply making out, the length of such activities can vary widely. Some people get bored rather easily with kissing, perhaps because they don't know many different types of kisses. By becoming familiar with the different kisses in this book, however, you'll be able to lengthen your necking sessions so that they last entire afternoons, entire evenings, entire dates. Ah, what bliss! What unending excruciating joy!

Advice for Men

Survey results reveal that in general women like longer kissing sessions than you do. As one man put it, "I don't like long kissing sessions too much, if it doesn't lead to something else I get bored." But if you kiss her for longer periods of time than you're used to, you'll be on the right track and you'll find she gets more aroused.

WOMEN:

"In my opinion you're wasting your time if you don't kiss for at least twenty minutes."

"Sometimes kissing (just kissing) lasts for an hour or two and continues through making love. Other times my lover and I will kiss all night and save making love for the morning."

"Ten to fifteen minutes is an easy stretch—fully clothed. But naked it is less. I like long kisses in places where you cannot *do* anything else."

"I usually engage in kissing for only about from two to five minutes with my husband before we have sex."

"I don't know how long, but I know I love to make out for hours."

"I have had marathon kissing sessions—like four hours—not one continuous kiss, but a very intense session. I enjoy this as long as it doesn't get routine."

"Some kisses have started all-night kissing sessions. One friend and I started kissing at nine P.M. and we kissed all night until three A.M."

"One time I kissed a friend for approximately seven hours—no foreplay, just fun kisses. It was excellent!"

The $\mathcal{P}$UBLIC KISS

They pass by and look and sometimes they even stop and stare and then they move on again and all the while you hardly notice because you've wandered off in your mind to a place where the palm trees are swaying in the breeze and the kisses are always sweet. Like shadows on a hot summer day when you haven't got a care in the world, these people who pass by while you kiss don't bother you at all. The crowd seems to melt into the background and all that's left is this delicious sensation as you and your girlfriend smooch on a busy sidewalk, in a ski lodge, or at the beach.

Yes, it seems that nearly everyone likes to kiss in public, and 94 percent of men and women tell us they've enjoyed doing it on occasion. But despite how sexually liberated we think we are in the United States, there is more public kissing in Europe, especially in Italy, France, and Spain. A young woman who visited a dozen European countries saw people kissing everywhere. "I studied in Germany for six months and my friends and I used to laugh about how intimate people would get in public. I don't consider myself conservative by any means, but what I saw stopped me in my tracks." According to another woman, "We should approach kissing the way Europeans do. French girls many times give oral kisses in public on the street or in a square or park and nothing is ever thought about it."

Kissing in public requires only a modest bit of courage. Usually no one interferes, although passersby may glance over to see what you're doing. In a crowded bowling alley one December a young woman told a boy that she wanted to kiss him because he was wearing Christmas colors. Then she kissed him in front of everyone. After that, both their games improved.

There are lots of good reasons to kiss in public and here are just a few:

- You simply can't wait to go somewhere private.
- You're saying good-bye at a train station or airport.
- You enjoy being affectionate and you don't care who knows it.
- You're at a party and other people are necking so you get turned on to the idea and do it too.
- You're an exhibitionist at heart and like to have an audience.

Let's be honest, we're all exhibitionists to some degree. And being seen is one of the chief pleasures of the public kiss.

How to kiss in public

1. Stand where people won't bump into you. Close to a building or at curbside are best.
2. Step up to your partner.
3. If she doesn't look receptive to a kiss, say something to clue her in to what you're going to do unless you want it to be a surprise.
4. Kiss her boldly but briefly.

Things to avoid in giving a public kiss

- Don't do it to excess so that other people feel uncomfortable.
- Don't get paranoid.
- Don't make an announcement to the crowd.
- Don't excuse yourself. Why should you? Virtually everyone kisses in public at some time or other.
- Don't grin and gawk at passersby after the kiss. If people look at you simply ignore

them. They may be picking up important pointers for use in their own public kisses.

Do you ever kiss in public?

WOMEN:
"I'm not timid about showing affection in public and it's fun to get caught. Sometimes I feel a bit like a show-off, sometimes special, sometimes embarrassed. I watch for my husband's reaction."

"Yes, I do kiss in public. One time my boyfriend came to pick me up from work and he rushed over to me and started to kiss me but I gave him only a peck. He wanted a longer kiss but I let him know I didn't want to. My boss was in the room. It was a very informal work setting and yet I was still uncomfortable. I generally like pecks in public although I do have fantasies about kissing him passionately in public. Passionate kissing is very private for me. I'll kiss passionately in a car or if I'm sure no one else is looking."

"Before I emigrated to the United States from France, I'd kiss in public at parties and it felt great."

"I prefer discreet, quick kisses."

"A particular man finally grabbed me in a restaurant (while we were enjoying a glass of wine and the tension between us) and kissed me very passionately. I was embarrassed *and* extremely excited. What was exciting was that his passion overrode any sense of his surroundings."

"In public places but not in public. I feel excited to steal a kiss in a public place—clandestine kisses are very exciting."

"I've grown up disliking other people's PDAS (public displays of affection), so I don't do it myself. On occasion I'll give a short kiss."

"I was brought up never to show *any* affection in public. But I have kissed in public anyway."

"I wouldn't want to make an exhibition in a public place. But if you were meeting your lover after a lapse of time, for example at an airport, it would be completely natural to kiss intimately and openly. I always enjoy being kissed in public."

"I come from England where we kiss instead of shaking hands."

"We never clinch kiss in public but we give each other pecks all the time."

MEN:
"Indulging on the dance floor (while dancing, that is) during a slow dance is . . . yum."

"I have kissed in public. Usually the girl is a little bit more embarrassed but I guess it could be the other way around. I never paid any attention to the people in the area, never noticed whether they stopped and stared. I don't generally mind if I see other people kissing in public. When I was in France I saw a lot more of it."

"Love to. Feel proud and somewhat sneaky. It's a way to proclaim to everyone that you dig each other."

Kissing Tip

Most people like being kissed in public as long as the kiss isn't too intimate or deep.

The wedding kiss

Your first kiss as husband and wife may be the most important public kiss you'll ever experience. Hundreds of people, scores of photographers and the eyes of history may be upon you at that moment. But there's no need to worry or lose your nerve. Take a quick look at the crowd, then kiss with these pointers in mind:

- Make it a kiss for you and the guests who are watching. The kiss should last a long time so that you give the photographers a chance to check the exposure and click away. Meanwhile you're kissing away.
- Men, don't be afraid to lean her back Hollywood style.
- Women, lean back like Scarlett O'Hara for a full photo.
- Choose the location for the first kiss beforehand.
- No French kissing—it doesn't show up on film and there isn't enough time to get warmed up for a French kiss.

"It wasn't memorable," said one nineteen-year-old newlywed. "He kissed me as we were leaving the church and there was nothing particularly romantic about it."

Many people said that their first kiss as husband and wife took place in a most uninteresting setting. To remedy this arrange for a romantic place that you'll remember for years to come. Try to have a professional photographer on hand to capture the moment. And make it a long soulful kiss that expresses all your feelings.

One woman who had her wedding kiss recorded on film said, "That photo summarized everything we felt for each other and has become almost a yardstick to measure all our subsequent kisses."

The Hollywood kiss

Next time you're on a date try the ultimate public display of affection—if you dare. This version of the public kiss requires a strong back and a desire to make a romantic fool of yourself. If you can do this kiss women will love you. Says one twenty-year-old, "When my boyfriend leans me back Hollywood style for a long romantic kiss it shows me that he doesn't care who knows we're a couple." The Hollywood kiss gets its name from the dramatic gesture you make when you almost sweep a girl off her feet and lean her back. The cover art for *Gone with the Wind* illustrates the technique. In one publicity drawing Rhett even picks Scarlett up in his arms. You needn't go to such extremes but it is essential to lean her back at an angle. You might have to get in shape at the gym before you can master this one.

To do a Hollywood kiss begin by grasping your date firmly around the waist. Then lean her back as far as possible. While holding her and leaning over her, press your mouth to hers and kiss passionately. Be careful not to drop her! At this point her head will be thrown back and she'll be totally at your mercy. Kiss her neck and make her giggle and keep her bent back until she gets dizzy from your kisses. If you do it right she'll feel like a movie star. I've seen many young men actually lean their girlfriends back at a forty-five degree angle. The sharper the angle the more onlookers will gape. Go beyond forty-five degrees and you'll stop traffic. But what if the girl is stronger? Then get her to lean *you* back.

The MUSIC KISS

Madison is twenty-two years old and she wears an iPod when she kisses because she kisses . . . to music. She's outside the library this afternoon waiting for her boyfriend Richard and she's listening through earphones to loud rock. When she spots his crew cut over the crowd of students her heart begins to pound like a tom-tom and she turns the volume down but not off to hear him say hello. Then they're alone behind the library surrounded by all the green of summer and the music fills her ears again.

In the inky glass doors she sees the reflection of her yellow MP3 player clipped to her shorts. With one hand she changes the track until she locks in on a love song that was very popular a few years ago, one with a strong beat so that when she puts both hands around Richard's waist she's kissing to that love song. She watches the red reflection of his shirt blend into the blond reflection of her legs in the glass as she kisses him. Richard is such a sweet guy and he kisses so divinely, his lips tender and soft and exploring. And as the music becomes more insistent he rocks her back and forth in his arms, kissing her with long breathless kisses that send shocks one after another over her body and through her blood until she's numb with a fainting feeling all through her nerves and through the extremities of her limbs. And then the music starts pounding in her ears, a new song about true love that she likes, and it takes her up and away and she rises on her toes to snuggle into Richard's kiss, going further and further into him as if drawn inward by the beating rhythm, lovely Richard with his crew cut and his sweet kisses that never seem to end—oh, how they blend into the music and make you go inside yourself and then outside yourself to that never-never land. She falls into the kiss like a rock sinking deeper and deeper into a bottomless pool until she's blind and unconscious and transformed somehow so that she knows that even when the song ends and she blinks open her eyes she's not going to be the same, she might not even be Madison anymore. Some part of her will always be lost in that kiss, lost in a fathomless pool from the bottom of which Richard is calling to her—Richard and the music together calling from the unseen depths.

By unleashing emotions, causing you to feel romantic and sexy, evoking moods you thought you'd never experience again, music can make your kisses rock. In fact, hearing music can make you feel pleasure ranging all the way from mild enjoyment to ecstasy. No wonder experienced lovers love kissing to music.

Once you discover how quickly melody and rhythm can lift your mood, you'll want to let the feelings evoked by music influence the sensation of at least some of your kisses. Whether it's blues or popular music on a Walkman, jazz or classical on a stereo, or a favorite tune on a car radio, 95 percent of people say that they occasionally listen to music while kissing. Only 5 percent claim it interferes with concentration, but boy they don't know what they're missing!

Now some daring music-minded souls don't just listen to music while kissing, they actually let its rhythm sink into their soul and move them so that they're kissing to the beat of a song. Done properly this type of music kiss is the most physically demanding technique in the book, but it will send you to another place and time and is well worth the effort it may take to learn it. The following instructions will introduce you to a whole new dimension in musical intimacy. And the beauty of the music kiss is you don't need musical talent to enjoy it. It'll work just as well for a musical genius as it will for a person who's tone-deaf.

How to do the music kiss

♫ Put on loud music.

♫ Stand face-to-face with your girlfriend.

♫ Keep your eyes open. You'll need to see where your kisses are going to land.

♫ Most popular music is played with a four-four beat. Kiss on the fourth beat. Wait three beats and then kiss again on the fourth beat. One . . . two . . . three . . . kiss! . . . one . . . two . . . three . . . kiss!

♫ After you get the hang of it, kiss on the second and fourth beat.

♫ Finally kiss on each and every beat. This requires lightning-quick reflexes and precise timing—but when the music gets into your blood there's nothing like it.

♫ Tilt your head slightly to the right for the first kiss, to the left for the second, etc. This way your noses won't bump.

♫ After a while add your own kissing syncopation by pausing for a few beats before jumping back into the regular rhythm. These pauses will surprise and delight your partner. In this way your kissing will become as unpredictable and fluid as music itself.

♫ Girls with ponytails can flip their hair from side to side with each kiss. This makes a music kiss look as good as it feels. Do this in a car! People will get jealous.

MEN:

"I like to kiss with background classical music. It's very pleasurable (if neither Bartók nor Ives)."

"Listening to music on a Walkman while kissing is like going to a Pink Floyd concert."

"I like kissing while listening to slow love songs on a Walkman."

"Yes, it can be a lot of fun and very sensual if it's the right kind of music, with crescendos."

"Sometimes you can kiss harder when there's a loud drumbeat."

"I like to kiss to Gloria Estefan in my kitchen!"

"When kissing I especially like slow and sensual music or fast and throbbing or sweet and melodic or sentimental. Or any kind."

"I listen to music when kissing in the car."

"Kissing with music is great because you have more desire, more emotions, you feel excited because you have the music inside and you feel inspired."

"I kissed once with a Walkman on and it was distracting. When my boyfriend had the same song on as me it was nice, but then we changed channels and I was listening to a love song and he was listening to heavy metal and it was weird."

The
ℐUPSIDE-DOWN KISS

Good kissers are always fantasizing about kissing in creative ways. In their imagination they toy with *all* the possibilities. And eventually they may begin to wonder, "What if I kissed my honey bear *upside-down?*"

Emily is that kind of creative soul. Twenty years old, infatuated with her second cousin Christopher, she's been flirting with him for two weeks. This evening she's with him by the pool. No one else is around. It's a strange and forbidden kind of pleasure she feels as Christopher lies back on a plastic chaise lounge and she sits beside him. He's so nonchalant and cool it's maddening!

She adjusts her one-piece bathing suit.

Now her hip is so close she can feel the warmth of his thigh. Ever so slowly she leans over him and their bodies finally touch. His brown eyes hold hers in a torpid stare that seems to draw her down toward him. Closer and closer she bends until finally their lips are touching and she can actually taste the chlorine on his mouth. She's kissing him at last!

But then her blood begins to run fast with the thought that she shouldn't be doing this. After all, he's her second cousin and even though she knows they'll never take it any further than a few harmless kisses, their families might object!

She breaks off abruptly.

"Stay put, Chris, I'm going to kiss you upside-down!"

He blinks up at her.

"Hunh? What are you talking about?"

"Just don't move. Keep your head where it is."

She gets up and goes to the back of the chaise lounge and stands there for a minute looking down at him. His brown hair is tousled, his dark eyes holding hers. But from this position—with his head totally upside-down in relation to her—he doesn't look like Christopher anymore! So she takes courage and bends down over him again. His mouth is so inviting from this angle! And he's looking up at her like a startled puppy. He could be anybody now. He sure doesn't look like her cousin. How free she feels now that his face is inverted! How excited she is as she kneels down at the head of the chair and kisses him upside-down!

Her head is spinning and her pulse races. His mouth feels so different! The upside-down kiss is perfect, absolutely perfect for moments like this when you're engaging in a semi-forbidden kind of kiss. The entire experience seems dreamlike and fantastic. His kisses are so new, so different! And it's the newness, really, that makes her heart pound. The newness and the feeling that at any moment they might be discovered. In fact she feels she might be discovered by *him* if she were to go back and give him regular right-side-up kisses. He might think twice about kissing her. If he saw her face the normal way he might remember that they're distantly related and he might want to stop. These upside-down kisses are saving her!

After a few minutes she's so excited she has to stop and catch her breath and *think* about what she's doing. In fact she may have to reevaluate her *entire life* now. Keep in mind that once you've tried a few upside-down kisses no normal kiss will ever feel the same. And any kissing part-ner will seem *extra special*. She steps back and looks down at Christopher's upside-down face. His dark moist eyes are like spilled ink, gazing dreamily up at her with a stunned expression that she can't decipher—because it's like no face she's ever seen before. It's upside-down!

The greatest pleasure of the upside-down kiss is this element of the new and the strange. Familiar faces suddenly become unrecognizable. It's the perfect kiss for lovers who've been married for years and who want to add some zest into their kissing. And if it adds zest for these lovers, imagine what it can do if you're just starting out in your relationship.

How to do upside-down kisses

1. Wait until your partner is lying down.
2. Kneel behind her.
3. Slowly lean over her until your mouth is above hers. Your upper lip will be directly over her lower lip, and your lower lip will be directly over her upper lip.
4. Move your head down until your lips touch hers.
5. Try a French kiss from this position. You won't believe how different it feels!
6. Break off now and then to gaze into her

eyes. Don't be surprised if you can't read her expression very well.

A young woman wrote to say she discovered this kiss when playing spin the bottle. Her boyfriend was standing over her and she was on the floor. He leaned over her and was face-to-face with her, upside-down. "He put his lips to mine and we were kissing. Then it turned into a French kiss. It was fun trying to kiss like that and finding tongues and all."

Some lovers who tried it found it awkward or uncomfortable. Because upside-down kisses are done from an inverted position it's important to maintain your sense of balance. The trick here is to select a good position for leaning over your partner. Kneeling on a bed can be a restful position. Try also lying on the floor and propping your chest up with pillows.

> **Kissing Tip**
>
> When your girlfriend sits down, stand behind her. If she looks up at you, lean down and give her a surprise upside-down kiss.

Dos and don'ts for upside-down kisses

- Do tell your lover how good he or she looks upside-down.
- Do switch positions so that sometimes you're lying down and your partner is leaning over you.
- Don't become confused just because your lover is upside-down.
- Don't worry about the fact that you have somewhat less eye contact with your partner in this position. Lack of eye contact will be more than made up for by increased tongue contact.

Did you ever kiss upside-down? If so, how did you like it?

MEN:

"It's not easy to accomplish anywhere but lying down, but definitely worth it. Particularly when tongue is involved . . . very strange sensation."

"I don't generally enjoy this kiss. It's too much like looking up the other person's nose."

"I've tried it and it's fun, playful, and silly."

WOMEN:

"This is a weird one. Unless you're just kissing someone's forehead briefly, it's very disconcerting. Usually one of us would turn around PDQ."

"I love upside-down kisses! They're the most outrageously fun types of kisses I've ever done. Definitely different and worth a try now and then."

"We were at a party and he was sitting and I was behind him, my arms around his neck caressing his hair and chest and his arms up along my arms stroking them, and then we held hands. On impulse I bent down and gently licked his earlobe and then touched my lips on the side of his face and then I looked down at him and he looked up at me and we French-kissed upside-down with me standing and him sitting, and we just kept going like that for two or three minutes."

Once you've mastered the upside-down kiss, you'll want to work a few of them into your kissing sessions whenever possible. Before you know it you'll be looking at people and wondering, just wondering, what they'd look like if they were standing on their heads. Wondering, just wondering, what those mouths would feel like if *you* were kissing *them* upside-down!

The SURPRISE KISS

Love is madness, isn't it? When two people are in love they lose their heads and act spontaneously, doing the craziest things to make each other laugh. If you keep your lover guessing she won't be able to predict what you're going to do next. Remember how Hannibal used the tactic of surprise to defeat the Romans. He crossed the snowy Alps on elephants! The defenders were so surprised they suffered a stunning defeat at the hands of the great strategist. So too will your sweetheart, not expecting your surprise kiss, fall like the Romans at Cannae, and in the battle of love victory will be yours. Inscribe within your heart the motto "I am the Hannibal of lovers" and you'll surmount all obstacles to romance because nearly 100 percent of men and women love surprise kisses.

How to give a surprise kiss

1. Wait for the right time. Just as Hannibal attacked when no one believed he could, so should you deliver your kiss when she doesn't expect it—early one morning, when other people are present, or maybe when you're shopping together.
2. Surprise her in a place where you usually don't kiss.
3. Use tactical distractions to enhance the surprise. Tell her she has nice earrings and then while pretending to examine them plant kisses on her neck and shoulder.

Do you ever like to surprise (or be surprised by) your lover with a kiss?

WOMEN:
"I like to surprise and be surprised with a kiss. It's an unexpected yet welcome show of affection. I feel special."

"Yes, I love both. I'll come up behind my boyfriend and kiss him on the neck and cheek. I've also done this and had this done to me during the middle of a conversation."

"When the relationship is new it's hard to know when the next kiss is coming. An old boyfriend kissed me quickly when he was introducing me to his friends for the first time. That made me feel so wonderful inside."

"Yes, sometimes I worry he's not thinking of me and then he'll come in and kiss me."

"One day I was in a clothing store alone. My lover walked up behind me and surprised me with a kiss on the back of my neck. It's still memorable after ten years."

"It's nice to be kissed unexpectedly when I'm lying in the sun on the beach or when I'm half-asleep and my husband wants to get me awake to make love."

"In the gym my lover walked across a crowded room of women and kissed me passionately while I was trying to do leg presses. He returned coolly to his weights. I continued exercising but my heart was thumping like a jackhammer."

"I love when he comes up behind me when I'm working in the kitchen and starts kissing me on the back of my neck."

"Yes—anytime, anywhere—magic. . . ."

"I absolutely *love* to come up to people I love from behind and give them a bear hug and kiss on the neck or cheek! I also love to wake up (or be woken up by) my lover with a kiss."

MEN:
"Yes, when you least expect it because it's crowded or not the typical time or place for a kiss."

"Yes, to say 'I love you' while dancing."

"Yes, first thing in the morning to wake my mate up—starting slow on the toes, or elsewhere, and ending on the lips."

"Yes, on the nape of the neck, usually. But softly on the lips as well."

"When you can't resist the temptation!"

The $\mathcal{V}$ACUUM KISS

Imagine that you're sitting with your boyfriend on the couch but neither of you is watching television. You're wearing a new silk blouse and he's told you three times this evening that you look stunning. Finally he leans forward to kiss you. After a few minutes you're necking seriously and you begin a long kiss during which your lips adhere tightly to his. Slowly and playfully and without even thinking about what you're doing you begin to suck the air out of his mouth. What a feeling! His lips taste like the inside of a peach and you draw his breath deep into your lungs until you feel your souls mingling. Then he begins to suck the air out of your mouth to the point where you've given him every atom of breath you have and you feel like you're so totally and completely his that your nerves are vibrating with shameless excitement. You've let him take your very life's breath away. How together you are at last! How mystically close! And on some level how profane and wicked it feels! Like Hylas in the pond with the nymphs, once you've acquired a taste for vacuum kisses they'll take you deeper and deeper beneath the surface until you're lost in all their breathless charm.

Types of vacuum kisses

In a double vacuum kiss you keep your lips sealed tightly together as you both suck the air out of each other's mouths simultaneously. Your cheeks may actually hurt from the intense pressure exerted on them.

In a reverse vacuum kiss you just touch your lips together—no tongue or teeth involved—and blow back and forth into each other's mouth.

In a mouth-to-mouth vacuum kiss you hold your partner's nose and then blow air into his lungs as if you were resuscitating him.

Kissing Tip

Eighty percent of your friends have never been vacuumed. I hope this is giving you ideas. Yes, it means this is the perfect kiss to spring unexpectedly on your boyfriend. If it doesn't work at first, tell him to breathe *out* while you breathe *in* and that should get things started.

Do you ever suck air out of your partner's mouth?

WOMEN:

"I hold his nose and blow air into his mouth so that it fills his lungs."

"Only someone I really know well."

"I've been married one year and I do this once in a great while. Sucking air out of your lover's mouth seems to be something done by new lovers, who tend to experiment more."

"Yes, he hates this."

"Yes! I also return the air. Sometimes it's only our lips touching—no tongue or teeth involved—and we're blowing back and forth into each other's mouth."

"It's not fun at all when done with a lot of force. But when done gently it can be enjoyable."

"It feels weird, but I like it. It takes quite a bit of practice."

MEN:
"It's very exciting to have this done to you."

"And how! If we're feeling really adventurous we play *chicken suck*—who can hold the pressure the longest! (We haven't turned blue ever, okay?)"

"It's such a turn-on. It's like she's giving herself totally to me when we suck air back and forth, and I can't think. I just love it."

"The vacuum kiss is a must! You simply suck the air out of your partner's mouth and watch them make a funny face."

"I hate when someone sucks the air out of my mouth. You can also blow air into someone's mouth. It kind of hurts but it's funny."

"It's different but sexually arousing. The partner who receives the kiss gets a blast of air in the beginning until the person runs out of air. Then it's a warm mist."

The $\mathcal{P}$ERFUME KISS

Chances are you've encountered this one on your own without even knowing it, perhaps like this. . . .

In the afternoon sunlight you check your curls in the mirror as you wait for your nails to dry. You're wearing blue cotton pants, a topaz-yellow blouse, white sneakers and matching yellow socks. You notice the time and run into your big sister's room and ask her frantically if she has any perfume you can borrow. She points to a little amber-colored bottle with a label written in a foreign language. She's talking as you splash it on hurriedly without even time to smell it or listen to her, and then you move.

You're out the door and halfway to the

street where Tommy's car is parked before the scent catches up with you. Hold on! It rises to your nose in slow insistent waves and you suddenly know you used too much. But you can't do anything about it now. *What did she say? It's a French perfume and it's stronger.* . . . Then you're sitting beside him, he's driving to your favorite picnic spot, and even though the windows are down you're constantly aware of this woodsy floral scent. What *was* that stuff? When he parks, the fragrance fills the whole car and you're mortified even as you notice that this smell has layers to it, luscious woodsy notes on top and beneath them a heavy musky fragrance that lingers like the refrain of a sad song. Tommy kisses you and as he does the odor seems to change, giving the impression that the air contains something like talcum powder. He inhales deeply, saying you smell delectable, delicious, sexy, naughty. And indeed you do. Suddenly you give yourself over to his kiss, and the fragrance which at first seemed merely musky now becomes pungent, almost imperceptibly the odor begins to resemble the emanations that rise from day-old underclothes. He's kissing you with a steamy passion and your senses are numbed as layer after layer of the intoxicating fragrance fills your nostrils and penetrates deep into your lungs. Your sister never prepared you for this! He kisses more insistently than ever, his lips wandering deep into the hollow of your neck, seeking the source of that deliciously intimate aroma.

So goes the perfume kiss, *a kiss in which any sensual odor plays a part*. But this is merely the start. It's a kiss with as many subtle variations as there are fragrances. Still, of the thousands of fragrances you can perceive, perhaps none is as exciting as the smell of your lover's hair or arms or neck. Indeed, throughout history the most passionate lovers have been those most sensitive to human smells. The emperor Napoléon loved the unwashed smell of his wife so much that he would write to her from the battlefield and tell her not to bathe for a week so that when he got home he could enjoy her natural body odor. When the poet Goethe traveled he took along his lover's bodice to be reminded of her scent. And when one of H. G. Wells's mistresses was asked what she liked about the overweight and unattractive writer she said he smelled of honey.

Many survey respondents said that the smell of their lover was often the greatest natural aphrodisiac, more powerful than any perfume. It's no surprise that perfumers often try to duplicate human smells and regularly use animal scents like skunk, civet, and musk to give a sexual tinge to their creations. Even some vegetable scents are sexually stimulating; the smell of yeast, baked bread, beer, fresh tobacco, cut grass—all act as mild aphrodisiacs, mimicking as they do some natural human scents.

Unfortunately, the majority of smells are anathema to modern society. It's even difficult to talk about the subject since our language has no words for most of the fragrances you can perceive. When you're told every day by advertisers that you must deodorize yourself and eradicate all body odors, you begin to get the message that natural smells are bad. So you'll probably have to coax yourself and your lover into trying the perfume kiss.

How to do the perfume kiss

1. If your girlfriend is wearing perfume breathe it in deeply before, during, and after each kiss.
2. Embrace her and inhale the natural fragrance of her hair, her sweat, her skin.
3. Kiss up and down her body, stopping at any interesting smells along the way. Be fearless about encountering strong smells but if you come across one you don't like simply move on to the next.

4. When you encounter a fragrance you *do* like, compliment her! Then keep on kissing.

Kissing Tip

Press your nose to your girlfriend's neck just under her ear—this is a spot where most women apply perfume— and sniff repeatedly and quickly like a dog on the scent until she cries with tears of laughter, then kiss her rapidly all over her neck and face.

Do you enjoy kissing a person who is wearing perfume?

MEN:
"Some perfumes are too overpowering but some are *very* nice."

"Yes, it adds another dimension. If the perfume is strong it repels me. If it's just enough to detect and only here and there it adds to a person's natural scent, which I usually enjoy."

"I love the way she smells! When I kiss her sometimes I'm like a hound dog, sniffing and kissing all over her body and getting turned on as I come across different fragrances, whether natural or artificial. I especially love putting my nose under her arms. Sometimes when she's going away for a while she'll let me borrow one of her shirts so I can be reminded of her by its musky scent. And I hate when she uses a deodorant because it kills all her animal magnetism."

"Her perfume sort of puts me in a daze. Soft and light is just great."

"I love the smell of bare skin, even sweat . . . mm."

WOMEN:
"I enjoy my husband's natural body odor."

"Perfume can increase my *intensity* and the type of kiss I deliver. It's exciting to move around the body and stop at a smell. This also applies to natural body odor. I have a very sensitive nose."

"I love kissing someone who's wearing fragrance."

"The smell of cologne can help stimulate arousal but it normally *tastes* lousy."

"A faded cologne on a man can be very pleasurable. It must be faded though. It has to be blended into his own scent, which hopefully is great."

"For me kissing is a five-senses type of thing and kissing a man who is wearing a good cologne is so exciting."

"I don't really like deodorants, talc, aftershave. The smell of a clean man is more than enough to drive me wild."

"Even when he isn't around and I smell that cologne I always smile."

"I have an extremely good sense of smell, so I always recognize events, people, etc., by their smell. I like cologne if it's had a chance to blend in with the person's natural scent, if it's not too strong and if it's constant (i.e., you smell that cologne and instantly think of the person). This might sound silly but fabric softener—Downy, Bounce, whatever—is the *best* cologne there is."

"I like recognizing the smell of a person."

"The natural smells of a person's hair, body, and mouth remind me of people a lot more than perfumes or other cues do. I remember a few months ago giving an old friend a long kiss and the comfort and memories it brought back were all wrapped up in the clean line-dried scent of his clothes and the familiar old lemony shampoo fragrance of his hair."

The ROLE-PLAYING KISS

Imagine that you're Cleopatra kissing Caesar in the great palace at Alexandria. Exotic incense wafts through the royal bedchambers, morning sunlight streams down from the high windows, and silk sheets await you and the ruler of the Roman Empire. What kisses you could kiss if you were king and queen of the Nile!

Or imagine you're a young woman living in the Old West and you're standing outside the bank on a hot afternoon. Suddenly a rider on a black horse appears in a swirl of dust. A moment later you're on the horse beside him. Now the two of you are galloping out of town. Your friends and neighbors stand staring in the street. The scent of gunpowder fills your nostrils. The horse slows down and finally you're alone with your secret lover—the outlaw from Dodge City. You get off the horse and he takes you by the hand and leads you under a tree. You look up into his eyes in the shadow of his black hat. With a sardonic sneer on his lips he takes you into his arms. No words are needed. You know what you're there for. No one can see the two of you now. But even if the world were looking, you couldn't stop yourself. Your heart is beating fast. The sun feels warm on the back of your neck. Yesterday is gone. Tomorrow doesn't matter. All that matters is what's in your heart, and that tells you to do only one thing.

Kiss him!

Kiss him and forget everything else. Kiss him as if you would die for him. Kiss him as if your blood and his were running together through your lips.

But kiss him!

Everyone has yearned to be someone

else, if only in dreams or daydreams. In role-playing, these fantasies can free your creative and emotional side, bringing fire and passion into kisses that would otherwise feel ordinary and dull. A role-playing kiss is any kiss in which you make believe you're someone else by introducing an element of pretense into the situation.

There's no limit to the different kisses and scenes you can develop. Don't worry about losing your mind or becoming someone else permanently. When the kisses stop and the dust clears, when the gold tables and silver jewelry vanish, when the FBI stops following your car, you'll be yourself again, same as usual—with only one difference: you'll have kissed a kiss the likes of which no one has experienced for hundreds, maybe thousands of years. Here are just a few of the role-playing kisses you can try:

Slave and master

Women:
"We pretend to be slave and master sometimes."

"Tell me what to do, overpower me, kiss me—bliss!"

"I've done this but not recently. It's a lot of fun but tends to push buttons!"

"There were occasions when I *felt* like a slave to someone. This giving-in can be luscious. But maybe, sadly, it's not pretend enough."

"In my head sometimes I pretend I'm a slave to him."

Men:
"No, I don't like that—but she likes to have me be forceful and be a real man."

"Sometimes we adopt exaggerated dominant and submissive roles, telling the other, 'Talk dirty to me' or demanding that the other reply 'Yes sir!' or 'Yes ma'am!' "

The androgynous kiss

Almost 80 percent of the people I surveyed found the idea of switching sex roles mentally while kissing—the androgynous kiss—difficult to even consider. But a young woman wrote to tell me she tried it with her boyfriend. "His reaction to the kiss when I pretended I was a man was basically, *Wowie!* It was very revealing to our relationship, provoking lots of conversation that continues."

If you're brave enough to try it you may gain some insights into how your partner perceives the whole kissing experience. The kiss is rather easy to do. You just mentally try to imagine what it's like to be a member of the opposite sex while kissing. You don't even have to tell your partner what's going through your mind.

Have you ever switched sex roles while kissing, pretending you're the opposite sex? Why did you do this and how much fun was it?

MEN:

"A strikingly attractive girl once surprised me by asking if she could put lipstick on me and when I agreed she started cooing about how beautiful *I* was! Then she put makeup on me and we switched sex roles while kissing. It was extremely erotic."

"I've discovered that many girls harbor an almost unconscious desire for the softness of a female in their boyfriend. My girlfriend occasionally likes me to wear a blonde wig and act feminine. It brings out my sensitive side and makes me kiss really sweetly. We both get turned on from it."

"Pretend? No. But there are plenty of role reversals! I enjoy being pursued and having the other take the lead as much as I enjoy pursuing. I feel a relationship has to be give-and-take. So sometimes she's in charge and doing the work and giving me pleasure and other times I do the work, give direction, etc."

WOMEN:
"I've occasionally switched sex roles while kissing just to understand what he's experiencing—and it's fun."

"Switching sex roles is very exciting and I learn more about myself and what I can do."

"I've wondered what it would be like to be a man kissing *me*. I've wondered this because I'd like to know if I'm a good kisser."

"I've done this but it wasn't cool. I'd rather have him take the lead."

"Yes—but this really requires trust—and is very challenging. Sometimes it's just in my head."

"I used to be very androgynous and had many friends of the opposite sex who were gay. I thought kissing some of them was magnificent."

"I did this and I liked it a lot. It let me see the world through the eyes of the opposite sex. It was daring and fun."

"I've tried to imagine I'm a man kissing a woman. Is that sick or what! . . . I've got the supposed upper hand—taking control of the kiss, handling the hair, jaw, etc. It's good."

The gangster kiss

The streets are almost deserted. You have one hand in your jacket pocket on your .38 automatic. At the curb Vito is sitting in a black Ford with the motor running. He's smoking a cigarette to calm his nerves. Your accomplice is looking up at the tall glass buildings that mirror the blue sky. You turn to her and notice a strange romantic gleam in her eyes. Perhaps it's only the reflection of the bank. She takes a breath to bolster her courage and her white teeth flash. Without thinking you bend down and kiss her roughly on the lips. Suddenly her mouth feels like the softest and most beautiful thing in the world. Your heart is beating fast, your head is swirling and you almost forget that in a few minutes you'll either be rich . . . or dead. You have just succumbed to the gangster kiss.

Because gangsters live outside the law they're not hampered by rules and restrictions; they live the way they want and enjoy a greater degree of freedom than most people. Their methods of kissing can teach you how to have fun and feel free. And since they often risk their lives, gangsters are usually filled with a high-strung anticipation and nervousness that can overflow into their sex lives and make their kissing urgent and erotic. They know they may be dead tomorrow and as a result they routinely kiss with a fervor that would sear the lips of the lawful.

Do you ever make believe that you are criminals?

WOMEN:
"Once at a costume party I dressed up as Al Capone and it was fun. When I kissed my boyfriend I laughed right in his face."

"The more aggressive you pretend to be the more passionate the kissing becomes."

"I pretend to be Madonna because she has a rebellious attitude. Sometimes I dress and act outrageously like she does."

"I sometimes make believe I'm the gangster's woman and I wear a really trashy dress. My boyfriend acts rough and it's an escape from the civilized world for me. No domesticated man can compete with him when he's that way."

The gangster kiss is by far the most creative type of kiss. It demands both a criminal's ruthlessness and a lover's sensitivity. It is one of the most formidable weapons in Cupid's arsenal and once you master its subtle intermixture of fact and fantasy your love life will never be the same. Every meeting with your sweetheart will be as memorable as a blackmail threat, every date as exciting as a conspiracy, every kiss as stimulating as a bank robbery.

The FRIENDLY KISS

Kissing is such a fun activity! It's a wonder more people don't do it with friends. . . . A friendly kiss occurs when people who aren't romantically involved give each other a kiss, whether on the cheek or lips. A young woman says, "There's another type of kiss between men and women, a kiss with little or no romantic meaning attached to it. I love to kiss my male friends when I can. I'm sorry more of them don't understand that a kiss can be a purely friendly gesture. Because men don't realize that a kiss *can* be just a kiss, they expect more when you kiss them. But that ultimately backfires and works against them because I'm afraid to kiss them in a purely friendly way."

Indeed the very idea of a friendly kiss seems to be impossible to many people. Says one young man, "On the lips? You don't know women. I never kiss women who are just friends on the lips or they'd become more than friends. I don't think a kiss can remain platonic. No kiss on the lips is strictly a friendly kiss—at least in our Western culture. And a kiss isn't just a kiss. To kiss a girl is like saying you love her."

Who is right? Can a kiss remain purely friendly, expressing good feelings and affection without overtones of sexuality and romance? Ironically, asking this question does more to obscure the truth than to shed light on it because it implies that the answer is either yes or no. The Polish mathematician and philosopher Alfred Korzybski cautioned that when we think of things in terms of black and white either-or distinctions—which we tend to do all too often—we miss the subtle truths which can be discovered only by observing the world itself.

In fact, when we look at what people actually do and experience we find that there is a wide spectrum of different kinds of kisses ranging from friendly to erotic, with every conceivable different level of intimacy in between. At one end of the spectrum are simple greeting kisses which are largely devoid of sexual overtones. Most often these are cheek kisses but occasionally they can be brief lip kisses. Then there are romantic and passionate kisses, which are almost always on the lips and may also occasionally involve the tongue. Once this range of different types of kisses is acknowledged, one can begin to calculate the number of kisses that fall into each category. It turns out that nearly 100 percent of people have experienced romantic kisses but only 36 percent have given friendly kisses to members of the opposite sex, usually in greeting but occasionally as an exercise in pure affection.

Kisses between men and women in our culture are almost always associated with romance. As a result most people forego the pleasures of kissing friends of the opposite sex. But when done properly a friendly kiss can be a pleasant experience and need not lead to deep romantic attachments. Sometimes it's even a way for friends to realize that their relationship will *not* progress further. Says an eighteen-year-old, "Kissing my best friend a long time ago was odd but very good. We were quite close and still are, just not in a romantic way. We slept together a lot (nonsexually) at his house but never did more than kiss twice. But it really wasn't attached to a romantic feeling. Once we kissed we realized that we were both more content not doing that."

Kissing Tip

This kiss could get out of hand unless you're careful to make sure it remains platonic.

How to keep a kiss platonic

1. Most people don't discuss whether a kiss is going to remain platonic. They simply kiss and hope for the best. It may help, however, to discuss the fact that you want the kiss to remain purely friendly.
2. Kiss your platonic friend in public so that there's less danger of the kiss leading to anything else.
3. Keep your first platonic kiss short and sweet.
4. Avoid open-mouth kisses.
5. Don't get too active with your hands during the kiss. In other words don't play with your friend's hair or run your hands seductively up and down her back.

> **Kissing Tip**
>
> Avoid French-kissing platonic friends. As one twenty-five-year-old male put it, "My one rule is—no tongue except with significant others!"

Our survey indicates that 91 percent of women and 80 percent of men are convinced that a kiss *can* remain purely platonic. Still, most people (64 percent) *never* attempt this kind of kiss. Of the 36 percent who do, most (95 percent) don't discuss whether the kiss is platonic or not beforehand. Men and women overwhelmingly agreed about one thing—*two out of three wish they had more opportunities to enjoy platonic kisses with friends of the opposite sex without having to feel pressured to move on to further sexual contact.*

Would you like the opportunity to kiss more members of the opposite sex without having to move on to other sex acts with them?

WOMEN:
"I do now. I know when someone is making more of a kiss than I am and I can usually disentangle myself from that situation right away. I'd like it if more men here in Canada thought kissing was a singular activity though."

"No. I like to lead into sex with kissing. If you're going to kiss me you'd better follow up with more later on. Don't start something you can't or won't finish!"

"It can be fun, yes."

"For those who can be platonic about their kissing, that's great. Kiss more people, start a revolution, life is grand. I think if more people kissed platonically the world would be much happier. Same goes for hugging."

MEN:

"I kiss anyone it doesn't bother. I'm a mad hugger too. My friends are close . . . there's no sexuality implied. Heck, I kiss my same-sex friends and so do my women friends."

"Sure I would, but to be honest I think after a period of time if it was a girl I liked a lot it would have to move on to other things."

"I truly believe kisses can remain platonic and I also believe that the more kissing of members of the opposite sex the better."

Do you ever kiss friends of the opposite sex (a "friendly kiss")? Can such a kiss remain platonic? Do you discuss the fact that the kiss is strictly a friendly kiss? Is a kiss just a kiss?

WOMEN:

"Yes kisses can remain platonic. It usually helps if both parties define how they see such activities. I tend to discuss it with people I kiss. Not all kisses are just kisses though. A lot of the time platonic kisses are a sort of testing ground in which you decide if you really are attracted to someone or if the relationship should remain on a friendship level. If someone makes a big deal out of asking me if they can kiss me, I *know* it isn't just a friendly kiss—there are ulterior motives behind the request."

"No. Hell no! So I don't even try it. I know I will want more. NO, NO, NO, NO. And still I say—NO!"

"No, I don't kiss platonically but if men kiss me on the cheek it is usually okay."

"I suppose a kiss can remain platonic, but then what's the point? Besides, I think it's usually such an intimate act unless it's directed to a family member that I wouldn't feel comfortable kissing a friend. In my opinion a kiss *isn't* just a kiss."

MEN:

"Yes, I kiss friends of the opposite sex platonically and I believe such kisses *can* remain platonic. We don't discuss per se the fact that it's platonic because there's little suspicion between us. If it will make someone uncomfortable I don't . . . but if not, I do it when I can."

"Some kisses are just friendly—no pressure, no tying emotion . . . some are so much more."

"When I kiss women platonically it is never on the lips."

"I sometimes give a friendly kiss. And yes, they can remain platonic. We don't discuss it. It's just assumed that it is platonic."

The SHY KISS

Most Westerners are always trying to earn more, do more, and be more. Sometimes I wonder why. And when I see two people from Japan kiss, I know there's another way.

Now, I mention Japan only because when I talk about the shy kiss the Japanese have the market cornered, so to speak. Japanese couples and Asians in general are much more discreet and circumspect about kissing, especially in public. Says one young woman from Japan, "Since coming to America I have tried to learn American customs, including kissing. I said to my husband, 'Why don't we try to become more like Americans and kiss more?' He got indignant and refused. 'I'm Japanese,' he said, 'not American.' So we don't kiss much. Back in Japan my mother would drop dead if she saw two people kissing in public—really no one kisses in public. She'll immediately turn off the television if the actors kiss."

Yes, indeed, there *is* another way. You could call it the Japanese kiss because it's so common in that country, but probably a better term for it is *the shy kiss* because it's really a way of kissing that's almost always adopted by the shy and the reticent no matter where they hail from.

You may not have seen this kiss yourself because it's usually done when people feel they're away from prying eyes. I first saw it by accident in a park when a young couple who thought they were alone did it on a summer's day, and I offer the technique here for your consideration with a promise that there is a method to their madness.

You begin a shy kiss by standing face-to-face at least a foot away from your partner. You're almost standing at attention, but not quite. Before doing anything else you turn your head and look left and then right to make sure no one is observing you. Your partner does the same. Then without saying a word and without even puckering up you both lean forward and touch lips. After a brief interval you stand back at attention, or almost at attention, and snap your head right and left to make sure no one saw you. Then you repeat the procedure.

"What good is the shy kiss?" I can hear some readers asking themselves. "It's so . . . *sexless!*"

Far from it! Strange as it may seem, the shy kiss is one of the most erotic kisses in the book. The element of holding back, of hesitancy, of Taoist simplicity—all this has its arousing effect. After you've been kissing for a number of years you're liable to become jaded. Nothing seems new anymore. Kissing loses its zing, its excitement, its stimulating qualities. But this is largely because you have been trying always to progress, when instead perhaps it is time to regress, to forget, to become the neophyte for a while . . . and kiss as the Japanese do.

The $\mathcal{T}$ROBRIAND
ISLANDS KISS

Here's a kiss your lover has probably never heard of—a kiss named after the South Sea Islands where it's so commonplace that everyone does it. The kiss was unknown in the rest of the world until 1929 when anthropologist Bronislaw Malinowski visited the Trobriand Islands (pronounced: TROW-bree-ahnd), investigated the local sexual customs, and wrote a marvelous account of his research, *The Sexual Life of Savages*. The Trobriand Islands are located about 1,850 miles due north of Sydney, Australia, in that part of the South Pacific Ocean known as the Solomon Sea. Malinowski found that the Trobriand natives consider our custom of kissing (pressing lips to lips) a rather silly and dull practice. But although they don't kiss as we define kissing, they do use the mouth during lovemaking.

Two lovers will typically begin by talking for a long time, grooming each other's hair and hugging and caressing each other. Then they rub noses just like the Eskimos. They also rub their *cheeks* together and then they rub mouth against mouth—without kissing. Next they suck on each other's tongue in a shameless variation of the French kiss and they rub their tongues together. As they become more passionate they bite each other's chin, cheeks, and nose. Next comes a critical part of the kiss—they bite and suck each other's lower lip quite vigorously, sometimes even drawing blood. Then they pull out handfuls of each other's hair. And finally they bite off each other's eyelashes. This custom of nibbling on their partner's eyelashes is a form of endearment usually reserved for the height of lovemaking. In fact, in the South Pacific it's a status symbol to have short eyelashes. It shows you're popular.

Many readers will understandably consider this type of kissing bizarre. But keep in mind that aspects of the Trobriand Islands kiss are already present in Western lovemaking to one degree or another. After all, we bite the lips, we scratch the back, we pull the hair. All we've got to do is chew on the eyelashes and we're kissing like proper natives.

How to do the Trobriand Islands kiss

1. Run your hands through your lover's hair.
2. Rub noses.
3. Rub cheek against cheek.
4. Rub your mouths together—without kissing!
5. Suck each other's tongues.
6. *Rub* tongue against tongue.
7. Suck your lover's lower lip *vigorously*.
8. Bite your lover's lower lip.

9. Bite your partner's chin and cheek.
10. Nip at your partner's nose with your teeth.
11. Thrust your hands into your partner's hair and pull forcefully.
12. Bite off your lover's eyelashes.

The Trobriand Islands kiss requires a wild and uninhibited nature. Practicing it may change you completely. But if you feel experimental, go ahead and set the ritual in motion. Let the savage in you free. Make tribal drums beat. And when your friends ask what happened to your eyelashes, simply smile and say, "Haven't you heard of the Trobriand Islands kiss?"

PART THREE

How to

French-kiss

$\mathcal{W}$HAT IS A FRENCH KISS?

The French kiss is the most intimate, sensual, and exciting kiss and yet up until now there have been no explicit descriptions of it for lovers to study. Young people interested in the French kiss, also known as the soul kiss or tongue kiss, have had to rely upon chance or luck in perfecting it. Typically lovers stumble upon the kiss accidentally while on a date. It might happen this way. . . .

You are sitting with your sweetheart on the couch. You had planned to take in a movie, but after her parents go out for the evening she suddenly suggests that you stay inside. She picks up a book of love poetry and wonders what you think of a certain poem by Tennyson. You lean over to read the poem. Suddenly you are sitting right next to her. The poem is entitled "Kisses." You look down at the page and begin:

> *Once he drew*
> *With one long kiss my whole soul through*
> *My lips, as the sunlight drinketh dew.*

You are just about to kiss her when she takes the initiative by moving forward to kiss you. What a pleasant surprise! You yield to her, becoming passive for a moment as she leads the way. You are so torpid, so easy, so yielding that as she presses her mouth against yours, your lips slowly part and her tongue slips inside your mouth for a moment. Now she is perhaps a bit shocked and she draws back.

"We better stop for a while," she says.

"No, no."

Now you kiss her, and as you do her lips open and your tongue slides lightly and effortlessly into the soft interior of her mouth. You can hear her breathing. You have forgotten to breathe yourself. Finally you remember to inhale through your nose so that you can prolong the kiss. Your heart is pounding and you feel you have broken through to new territory—and indeed you have. You think you have been perhaps too aggressive. But your fears are allayed when you feel her tongue meet yours. Her mouth feels and tastes so delicious as your tongues twist about each other. And now her tongue pushes slowly and deeply into your mouth. She is so bold, almost brazen in her exploration.

There are no words that can adequately describe the sensation of a good French kiss. Suffice it to say that you have now reached an advanced stage of kissing that can lead to almost symbiotic closeness. Handle this kiss with care and it will pay you rich dividends. You will get to know each other in a new and intimate way for the French kiss can bring you even closer than the act of sex.

Her family was expected back in two hours. Can you believe it, here they come now! How can it be? Have two hours slipped by so quickly? Your heart is still beating fast as the two of you move slightly apart. But you feel that you are still in contact with her. Somehow the French kiss has brought you so close together that for hours and days afterward you will feel different toward each other. It's as if a mystical connection links the two of you together. Ah, the delight of it! Ah, the secret thrill!

Do you like French-kissing?

Ninety-six percent of men and women said they liked this kiss at least some of the time, making it one of the most popular forms of kissing.

WOMEN:
"When I think of French-kissing, one man in particular comes to mind. His French

kisses weren't sloppy or overly wet. They were penetrating. He used to play chase with his tongue and my tongue in such a way that I wanted it to never stop."

"Very much—you feel like you're melting into each other."

"I like the speed, depth, unification with the other."

MEN:
"The more tongue the better!"

"I like deep, fast, hard tongue kisses."

"The French kiss I could do for hours. I place one hand on the girl's lower back and the other by the side of her head and play with her hair. I breathe with my nose and playfully stick my tongue in and out of her mouth, licking her lips and sucking the air out of her mouth."

"I don't enjoy wide-open wet exploring. I like to French with the mouth only slightly open and prefer a softer, more gently probing kiss."

"When I was first kissed this way I felt in some sense violated. I didn't want anybody putting anything of theirs in anything of mine! If I'd been asked I would've been more receptive, but I wasn't and it seemed a bit gross. After a few times and some weeks I got the hang of it but it's not my favorite form. I do enjoy having someone run her tongue along the sides of my teeth up around the gums. I don't enjoy the stabbing, penetrating, rigid-tongued kiss. I like the fooling-around kind of kiss, a little dance kind of kissing."

Why is it called a French kiss?

The term *French kiss* came into the English language in 1923 as a slur on French culture, which was thought to be overly concerned with sex. In France it's called a *tongue kiss* or a *soul kiss* because if you do

it right it feels like your souls are merg-
ing.

What if I've never done
it before?

Some young people who have never kissed
before worry about their first kiss and
think, What if it turns into a French kiss?
How will I deal with it? And what if my
partner can tell it's my first time?

First of all, let me assure you that it's
impossible for anyone to know it's your
first kiss or your first French kiss. They'll
never know unless you tell them. If you've
never kissed before just keep your mouth
closed during your first kiss. If the boy
tries to stick his tongue into your mouth
before you're ready, pull back gently and
stop kissing. "Wait a minute," tell him.
"You're moving too fast." But if you'd
like to try it, open your mouth and play
chase back and forth with your tongue
and his. If it gets to be too much you can

always gently lean back and close your mouth to end it. Gasp a little and push him away. He'll get the message. Remember you always have the option of saying, "Let's take a break," so don't hesitate to slow things down if he's going too fast.

In summary, the French kiss is the most popular kiss because it is the most exciting. Even young people who have never French-kissed begin to dream about it as this comment from a fourteen-year-old humorously demonstrates. "The person I was kissing was sitting on the bus seat and I was right next to him and I gave him a quick kiss but then all of a sudden I just had the idea to do something with my tongue, and I licked Taylor on the side of his cheek! And it was a big lick too! I guess I was in the mood for French-kissing but had to show my feelings some other way."

WHAT CAN GO WRONG DURING A FRENCH KISS?

Lucky the kisser who hasn't had an occasional bad experience! And when French-kissing, the number one complaint is breathlessness. Sometimes you'll have a partner who's just a little too enthusiastic with his tongue. Says one girl, "When I turn blue he doesn't realize it means I need to breathe!"

If his tongue is too invasive, push him back gently and make a joke by saying something like, "Wow, your tongue!" Then ask him to go a little easier with it.

But breathlessness can also be caused by improper technique. The correct way to French-kiss, of course, is to breathe through your nose. Not only will this solve most breathlessness issues but it will also enable you to do much more intimate French kisses.

The second thing that can go wrong is that you might gag if your partner's tongue pushes down on the back of yours. The best way to avoid the gag reflex is to make sure your partner doesn't stick his tongue too far down your throat. If he does, tell him to stop or you'll report him to the kissing police. When you make a joke out of it, most guys will take the hint.

Another problem that annoys many girls is a French kiss that's too wet. "I get a lot of boys who are too sloppy," says one fifteen-year-old. "I wish they'd practice swallowing with their mouth open so they know how to not have a ton of spit." Naturally one should follow the Golden Rule in kissing and *do to your kissee as you would have her do to you.* In other words, the polite thing to do is swallow your own saliva. But keep in mind that the more intimate a kiss the wetter it's likely to become. If you're really into a kiss, a little wetness probably won't bother you.

The final problem you may run into is the mechanical kisser. Some people, for instance, will dart their tongue in and out of your mouth like a jackhammer. Others will suck your breath too much. "Every time she French-kissed me she'd suck the air out of my mouth and lungs in a frightening vacuum kiss," says one young man. "She would also suck my tongue, my lips, anything she could find." Some people have such strongly ingrained habits that it's impossible to change their behavior. The most you can do is remember to set a good example by putting some finesse into your own French-kissing and hope they follow suit.

How to Practice a French Kiss

Yes, you can actually practice a French kiss in the comfort and privacy of your own home. And you don't even need a partner to do it. That's right. You could practice on a picture in a magazine. You could practice on a doorknob. But the best way to practice is to use your imagination.

"Oh, that sounds dull!" you say?

Nay, nay, dear reader. If you have a good imagination an imaginary French kiss can keep you up nights. But don't practice on an imaginary lover. Not at all. Do as the great artists did. When Faulkner wrote his Nobel Prize–winning novels, did he invent people out of thin air? Not on your life! He usually had real people in mind as the models for his major characters. So when you practice I want you to practice like the greatest artists. Imagine you're kissing that special someone who fires your imagination and keeps you up nights tossing and turning in your bed with passionate thoughts of love. I want you to conjure up in your mind the image of this lovely sweetheart's mouth, and I want you to imagine kissing it gently at first then more insistently. And then I want you to imagine she opens that mouth and your tongues touch. Go through the entire kiss in your mind. What will you do? Will you retreat in embarrassment? Will you play chase with your partner's tongue? Will you run your tongue along hers? This is the best way to practice because it will prepare you for the real French kisses that lie ahead for you. And as you practice remember that you have the innate ability to become a great kisser.

Which is why I want you to know about another way to practice, a method that has helped many romantically minded people just like you. It may sound silly but it really works. Here's what you do:

1. Make a fist with your left hand.
2. Put your right thumb through it, to represent the tongue.
3. You can practice a French kiss on your hand!

In fact, it's so realistic, you could get turned on from it! "Oh, that thumb! That thumb! Honey, you gave me too much thumb!"

How to practice with a mirror

And now we come to one of the most effective ways to practice a kiss—with a mirror. This takes some getting used to. But it will work wonders for you if you're just starting out kissing and even if you've been kissing for years. The technique is to lean in and actually kiss the glass. Imagine that your lips are your partner's lips. How luscious they look! How absolutely inviting! You just can't resist! This may sound slightly narcissistic but the point is it works. You'll be getting the benefit of practicing without the fear of making mistakes, and you'll see how a kiss looks close-up.

How can you practice a kiss?

WOMEN:
"You might be able to practice a kiss by using a guy friend who's a really good best friend."

"I think a good way to practice is to begin by reading over some info on the type of kiss you want to do."

"I told my boyfriend that when we turn sixteen he could practice kissing with me. He started to laugh and I kissed him and then told him to try different kisses on me. He stopped laughing right away and started practicing. And we both discovered how much fun practicing can be!"

WHY DOES A FRENCH KISS FEEL GOOD?

There are two reasons why a French kiss feels good. The first has to do with human physiology and the extraordinary number of pleasure-sensing nerves in the tongue. Some of these are taste buds which can make a kiss taste sweet. In fact, taste receptors are also present in the lips and roof of the mouth—and if that doesn't give you ideas I don't know what will! . . . The point is you can actually use your lips to taste your partner during a kiss. Indeed, the tongue and lips have more nerve endings than any other parts of the body. That's why when you French-kiss you feel like your entire world has focused in your mouth.

Another reason a French kiss feels good

is because it's a childish thing to do. As mentioned previously, it's actually baby-ish. "Well, why should I do something babyish?" you ask. The answer may sur-prise you. Some species regress to a baby-ish state when they make love. For example you'll see horses nuzzling their faces to-gether in a way that mimics their infantile behavior with their mothers. Humans are among the species that regress when they fall in love. We even go so far as to call each other "baby." Regressing is a funda-mental part of human love-play and noth-ing is as infantile as a French kiss during which lovers regress to the earliest stage of psycho-sexual development—the oral stage.

So go ahead and regress. You'll find it's one of the most exciting things you can do when you're together with . . . your special baby.

How long should a French kiss last?

The length of a French kiss can vary but in general a French kiss should last longer than a lip kiss. Your first French kiss, however, might last only a few seconds or so. That initial tongue contact might even surprise you and cause you to stop quickly and pull back. A subsequent French kiss could easily last half a minute or forty-five seconds. A kiss of this duration requires you to breathe through your nose.

Once you get comfortable with the techniques and pleasures of tongue kisses, you'll be able to do even longer French kisses. Says one young man, "A good French kiss could last anywhere from a minute to three or four minutes." Amorous couples report that their French kisses sometimes last four or five minutes—or longer! And long French-kissing sessions can make you feel pleasantly dizzy and euphoric for up to four hours afterward.

This is the result of the production of endorphins, natural morphinelike painkillers released in the brain while kissing. Isn't it nice to know that French-kissing produces a natural and perfectly safe high? As if you needed more reasons to French-kiss!

Why do you like French-kissing?

WOMEN:
"The first time my boyfriend's tongue touched mine I was afraid my mouth was unraveling. I couldn't believe what I was feeling, it was so sensual and intimate."

"I think French-kissing is a great opportunity to get in touch with your partner's kissing preferences. Therefore, I usually approach French-kissing kind of experimentally, maybe playfully darting my tongue in and out of his mouth and then seeing what kind of reaction I get. That's the fun of French-kissing—it's very flirty and light."

MEN:

"What I like about French-kissing with my girlfriend is that intimacy, the feeling that the two of us are together. There's nothing that brings us closer."

"It gets me more excited than any other kiss."

"French-kissing makes me feel good while we're doing it and also for hours and days afterward."

How do i get boys to french-kiss me?

If you're a girl who likes to French-kiss you may occasionally find yourself dating a fellow who doesn't give you enough tongue. There are any number of reasons for this problem. Some guys are simply too inexperienced in the ways of kissing. Others are too shy. Still others have an aversion to touching tongues.

But don't give up hope. There are things you can do.

First, you should share your copy of this book with your lover. Reading it will serve to inspire him to try a French kiss more often.

Second, you must kindle within him a love of French-kissing by gently introducing your tongue into his mouth when you get the opportunity. But don't overdo it. You want to train him slowly to love what you love, and the best way to do that is to proceed intermittently.

Third, find out what kind of candy he likes. If it's Life Savers, buy some and have them on hand when you go out. If he chews gum, make sure you carry a package of his favorite brand when you go on a date. Almost everyone has one or more oral fixations—some smoke, some like lollipops, some like to chew the tips of their pencils. Find out through careful observation what your boyfriend likes and then encourage him in his fixation. Ever so subtly you'll be teaching him to like the same kinds of sensations that you enjoy when French-kissing.

Fourth, when watching a romantic movie in which an actor does a French kiss, say something positive about it to your boyfriend, such as "I'd love to be kissed like that!"

Fifth, as a last resort tell him that you'd

like to French-kiss more. But tell him when you're *not* kissing. If you try these suggestions you're bound to get more French kisses from him.

How do I get boys to *stop* French-kissing me?

Many girls worry about how to get boys to *stop* French-kissing them. They're afraid that their boyfriend will be too aggressive with his tongue. Or they worry about gagging or suffocating during a kiss.

Incredible as it may seem, some guys are just not observant enough to realize that they're suffocating you or making you choke! So it pays to have some tricks up your sleeve to get him to slow down.

The first thing to keep in mind is that it's very easy to stop a boy from French-kissing you. . . . What can you do if he's overdoing it with his tongue? Let me give you a big hint. His tongue is right between your teeth. See what I'm driving at? All you have to do is gently bite his tongue and he'll immediately stop.

Of course a much better solution is to talk to him and make him realize that he's giving you altogether too much tongue. Don't hesitate to tell him to go slower. And it's better to talk about it when you're not actually kissing. His ego might be bruised if you break off from a kiss and tell him he's not doing it right. So wait for a time when you're not kissing and mention it then.

How do I get girls to French-kiss me?

If you'd like your girlfriend to French-kiss more often there are some very effective things you can do. The first technique is to talk with her when you're not kissing and ask her point-blank whether she likes French kisses. I bet she'll say she's afraid she's going to gag or suffocate. If she has these common fears reassure her that you'll go slowly.

Try the French-kiss hand game. You ask her to touch her finger very softly to the tip of your finger. You tell her that's how gently you're going to French-kiss her. Believe it or not, most girls will get excited just to touch the tip of your finger. (The secret reason for this is that the fingers have almost as many nerves as the tongue.)

Another technique to get more French kisses is to tell her to make a "mouth" with her hand (as described on page 276). Then you kiss her hand. Suck her thumb a little, but do it ever so gently! This will make her see how much fun a French kiss can be.

Finally, remember to give your girlfriend room to breathe when French-kissing. Don't French-kiss her for too long initially. Try a short French kiss now and then. And wait for her to respond with her own tongue. Most importantly, let her lead sometimes during a French kiss. In other words let her push her tongue into your mouth while your tongue retreats back deep into your own mouth. This will build up her confidence and make her want to French-kiss you more frequently.

WHAT SHOULD I DO WITH MY TONGUE?

Your tongue is the most flexible part of your body. Next time you're in front of a mirror observe how you can make it pointy and sharp, curl it up longitudinally and latitudinally (if you can), flatten it out, and flicker it like a snake. Once you discover how many shapes you can make you'll naturally be eager to try them while kissing.

You can also use your tongue to read your kissing partner's mood and state of mind. Says one young woman, "I like to get a sense of how he's feeling through his tongue. It's amazing but when we touch tongues I'm sometimes convinced that I can read his mind. When he pushes hard I sense he's being very masculine. Then sometimes he'll let me take the lead and I know he's being more accommodating."

Of course one of the most pleasant things you'll do when French-kissing is lick your partner's tongue. The following quotes will help you do this along with the best of them.

Did you ever lick your partner's tongue? What was this like? Do you have any suggestions for how to enjoy this type of kiss?

MEN:

"It's a requirement to get to the more deeply intimate forms of kissing! Everyone literally does it differently, from slow languid tongue massages to fast-and-furious tongue tangles. If it's the first time go slowly and really feel the sensations. Run circles around her lips (where yours meet) then around her tongue. For something different go for the gum-cleft in front . . . or tickle the roof of her mouth (very ticklish there)."

"Yes, it feels very smooth and good. Let your tongue search out hers."

"I've done it and the tongue felt nice and smooth . . . until I got to the top of the tongue. Then it felt quite rough. To enjoy this kiss stay to the sides of the other person's tongue."

"What I like about licking her tongue is the intimacy of being so close to someone."

"It can be nice to lick her tongue but you have to know your partner very well to be comfortable with it. And it helps for her to be quite relaxed."

"Dueling tongues is one of the most pleasurable parts of kissing. I like to examine all the parts of my partner's mouth with my tongue and have her do the same with mine."

"Licking your partner's tongue feels great!"

"Take it easy and make sure the kiss is balanced. This type of kiss is very enjoyable but not if one partner is down the other's throat and the *quiet* partner feels overpowered. You need to work carefully, approach slowly, and stay in control. Frequent stopping to swallow saliva and to catch one's breath is also advisable. Being somewhat evasive adds to the fun— i.e., quickly licking your partner's tongue and backing off to wait for a response."

WOMEN:
"It's great once you and your partner figure out each other's rhythms and techniques. For people to whom this may sound gross, I suggest keeping an open mind (as in everything) and try it. They'll never say no again."

"I have licked my lover's tongue. It was slippery but also had tiny bumps."

"I like licking his tongue. I think people will either enjoy it or not. I suppose that one might learn to like it if one practices learning to enjoy it at a comfortable rate."

"Great French-kissing requires a certain amount of licking. The thing to do is relax and don't think your tongue has to be a plunger or anything. Start slowly or your partner will feel like you're eating them, not kissing them."

Advanced French-kissing

Under the cloak of anonymity your friends and neighbors confessed exactly what they like when French-kissing, and each of these suggestions is something you can do too.

- Twist your tongue around hers.
- Wrestle with her tongue.
- Playfully lick the tip of her tongue.
- Play chase back and forth with her tongue.
- Lick the inside of her lips while your mouths are pressed together.
- Repeatedly lick her tongue while it's in her mouth.

- Lick the roof of her mouth.
- Gently, then vigorously, suck her tongue.
- Gently chew on her tongue.
- Explore her teeth and gums with your tongue.
- Press your tongue forcefully against hers.
- Let her take the lead and follow her tongue. In other words playfully try to make your tongue pursue hers without losing contact.
- Press your tongue against hers as you simultaneously give her a hug.
- Sharpen your tongue into a narrow point and seek out the tip of hers.
- Spell out the alphabet or your partner's name with your tongue.

Variations on the basic French kiss

What specific techniques do you use in French kisses? What subtle variations have you experienced in tongue contact during French kisses?

WOMEN:

"Once in a while I'll playfully bite his tongue and suck it and run my tongue along his teeth. I explore his mouth as if I lived in there."

"I think starting slow and not just shoving your tongue down someone's throat works best. It's all about discovering a mutual rhythm. And not necessarily having lip contact while you French-kiss is good too."

"Variations: Rolling your tongue around the other's, exploring the roof of their mouth or their teeth, using your tongue to get the other's lip, and tongue wrestling."

"There are tons of variations—gentle slow darting tongues that lick your lips and then move into your mouth, twining tongues, sucking tongues. . . . Some people are really aggressive and you just take a submissive role and let them probe your mouth.

Other times you're aggressive and lead all the tongue play. It can be really playful, sensuous, passionate, anything at all."

"I love to tongue wrestle. I have had him bite down on my tongue slightly as I'm working it in and out. And of course I return the favor."

MEN:
"Twisting my tongue around hers and playing with the sides of a woman's tongue and, yes, licking the top of her mouth with my tongue—gets 'em every time! Some women have tried to play with the tip of my tongue and I like that."

"I like to take the tongue and suck it into my mouth."

"I just sort of walk my tongue around, licking her tongue and teeth."

"My mouth is open only very slightly and my tongue is not inserted very far."

"Gentle fluttering of the tongue . . . circling . . . slow gentle movements . . . no darting for the back of the throat."

"I just move my tongue around a lot, which works okay for me. I like the twirling-tongue-around-the-mouth technique."

"Move slowly. Alternate keeping your tongue firm and really soft. Pay attention to the tip of your partner's tongue, play with it. Lubricate lips from the inside. Light rubbing is exciting! Extended French-kissing might require ingenious ways of saliva disposal."

How can i improve my french kisses?

Kissers of all experience levels often ask how they can improve their French-kissing skills. Once you've mastered the basic moves, what more can be done? Is there anything else to do? A true kissing connoisseur will answer, "Yes, you can improve your technique!"

One of the best ways to improve your technique is to find out what the opposite sex likes. Despite the fact that the French kiss is the most popular kiss in the world, few people realize that there are significant differences between men and women when it comes to the use of the tongue. But if you take the following advice to heart, you'll always know how to thrill your kissing partners, and keep them coming back for more.

What do men like when French-kissing?

Research shows that when it comes to French-kissing, men like three things. First they like women to open their mouths more. This is easily accomplished. When kissing, open your lips wider now and then. This doesn't mean you have to keep your mouth wide open all the time when kissing. It simply means that you occasionally open your lips while kissing and keep them a little wider apart than you may be used to. The reason guys like this is that it gives them a chance to begin a tongue kiss with you and explore your mouth. In other words they'd like you to invite them in by opening up a bit more.

The second request guys make is that women take a little more of the lead in French-kissing. You can do this in any number of ways, such as initiating the French kiss now and then, using your tongue more, being more aggressive about pushing your tongue into his mouth, and moving your tongue in an exploratory way.

Finally, men have requested that you put some finesse into your French-kissing. Try to sense your partner's mood and French-kiss him back to match his

Advice for Women

If you want to excite a man, open your mouth more when kissing so that he can French-kiss you. Most men would also like it if you initiated more French kisses. And they especially want you to be more aggressive with your tongue, probing deeply into their mouth and taking an active part in keeping a French kiss going.

feelings. For example, if he's giving you gentle tongue contact, be gentle in return. If he's being more insistent press back against his tongue with more force yourself. In this way you'll be in tempo with your partner and your French kisses will take on all the romantic mystery of a dance of love.

What do women like when French-kissing?

Women love you to begin a French kiss in a sensitive and gentle manner. This means test the waters. Give her a little tongue and see how she reacts. If she doesn't touch your tongue with gusto or if she retreats her tongue back into her mouth, it's usually a sign that she's not ready to progress to a French kiss. If you respect her wishes by sensing this intuitively from her body language and tongue language, she'll consider you supremely romantic.

Women also like it when a guy can take the lead in French-kissing, just like in dancing. But they like it even more when you can relinquish the lead now and then and let them take charge. Just be a little less forceful with your tongue and try to sense her wishes and the direction she wants to go with her tongue. Follow her lead. When she pushes, you retreat. When she retreats, you follow gently, ever so gently. She'll love the fact that you let her take control occasionally.

Another thing a woman appreciates is a guy who is aware of her breathing. One out of three women reported being afraid of a French kiss because of bad experiences with guys who suffocated them. The responsible thing to do while kissing is to keep your ears attuned to her breathing. (When you're up so close to her, you'll actually be able to hear her breathing in and out.) Make sure she's able to breathe through her nose while you're kissing.

You'll score big points with your date if you don't suffocate her!

A related concern of gals of all ages is that they want to be able to French-kiss without gagging. They want you to use your tongue more in the *front* of their mouth, up near the teeth and the tip of the tongue. You can explore the roof of her mouth but don't shove your tongue down the back of her throat. That will make her choke and turn her off. If you've ever had this done to you, you'll know what I'm talking about. Guys can learn about the problem of giving too much tongue by trying this simple test. Next time you're brushing your teeth, brush the very back of your tongue where it goes down your throat. You'll gag. Remember the sensation and what caused it, and that will help you avoid this mistake while kissing.

Your girlfriend will also love it if you gently pat her cheek with your fingertips. The simultaneous sensory input from a

French kiss inside her mouth and finger-tips outside on her face can produce a combination of delightful nerve impulses which is likely to leave her feeling pleasantly dizzy.

Most women also like it when you take a break now and then from French-kissing. This could mean stopping kissing altogether for a few minutes or it could mean kissing her without any tongue for a while.

A final thing every woman really likes is when the guy gets very sensitive to how she's kissing him back. One woman said she likes her boyfriend to "listen" to the way she kisses, which means she wants him to reply to her tongue action with a similar tongue action. When she goes fast she wants him to match tempo. When she signals that she wants you to be gentle—by retreating or by becoming less forceful herself—she wants you to match her gentleness.

Advice for Men

If you're like most guys, the biggest mistake you make is putting your tongue too far down her throat. If she's reluctant to French-kiss, it may be because a previous boyfriend made her gag or suffocated her. Come right out and ask if she'd like you to lighten up. And keep your tongue in the *front* of her mouth. She'll be glad you did—and so will you.

Women's advice for men

Women report that although they like the French kiss, their partners resorted to it too often, were unimaginative, didn't move their tongues enough, or were too aggressive (initiating French kisses too early in a relationship). The number one complaint, however, was that guys put their tongues too far down their throat.

Their advice for men is to go slower, don't French-kiss on the first (or even the second or third) date, be gentle, try to sense your partner's mood and respond in kind, and most important of all *keep your tongue in the front of her mouth up near her teeth and lips*. Says one young woman, "If you allow the girl to breathe your French kisses will be a lot better."

"Men seem not to know any other way to kiss. It can be okay at times, but not *every* time."

"I don't like a lot of tongue. I really hate kissing someone for the first time and having their tongue go down my throat."

"Don't fish-mouth! Some guys feel like they have to completely overtake your mouth with theirs . . . yeech! And *listen* to your partner. If they're kissing you in a certain way, chances are that's how they want to be kissed back."

"Slow down! Your tongue doesn't have to dart furiously in and out of my mouth. Take your time, tease a bit, let me get my tongue in your mouth once in a while."

"Don't shove your tongue into your girlfriend's mouth too quickly and don't go too deep."

"I like French-kissing if it's soft, sensual, and intimate—as long as it's not slobbering or deep throat. Gentle delicate French kisses deepen intimacy."

"I like it but not when I feel suffocated by the person's tongue. I like light French-kissing."

"Sometimes it's invasive if you're not in a serious or long-time relationship."

"If the other person just wiggles his tongue it's no good. There needs to be passion and sensuality. I hate being sucked or swallowed by kissing."

Men's advice for women

"Put more passion into your French kisses. Touch me with your hands if they're free."

"Don't use your tongue as a dart!"

"Take things slowly. Let the kiss expand into a French kiss *if* it can. Sometimes it just isn't appropriate."

"Just get into it and breathe through your nose if you have to or breathe through the corner of your mouth."

"Enjoy the sensitivity, the intimacy. Slow and steady! Our tongues don't have to *fight!*"

Is there anything you don't like about French-kissing?

WOMEN:
"I don't like the fact that some guys misinterpret it as an invitation to go further. I see French-kissing as just a normal part of kissing but a lot of men think I'm overly

forward and that tongues involved means groping is allowed as well."

"When it's sloppy and really wet."

"I don't like when saliva gets all over my face."

MEN:
"I don't like it when *all* a woman wants to do is French-kiss. What about some variation, some soft kisses?"

"Unshared garlic . . . if she has had some and I haven't—ouch!"

"Tongue-gagging, wide-mouth, slobbering kisses. Yuk!"

What are some French-kissing games we can play?

Next time you're with your sweetheart, play doctor and tell her it's time for her test. She has to close her eyes and open her mouth. Explain that she's got to identify the object in her mouth with her eyes shut. The object, of course, will be your tongue.

Another game is to ask your sweetheart to spell out a word for you with the tip of her tongue. See if you can figure out what word she's spelling. You may have to stop after every letter to catch your breath.

You can also set a stopwatch and try to French for four or five minutes straight without breaking tongue contact. Now, if you find yourself getting excited simply thinking about these games, just wait until you play them. . . .

Dos and don'ts of French-kissing

Do:

- Take an active part in the kiss. Push your tongue into your partner's mouth. It may feel funny at first but you'll get over your shyness in no time.
- Relinquish control of the kiss now and then. When your girlfriend pushes her tongue

into your mouth, relax and enjoy the sensation, meeting her tongue with yours. Let her take the lead and without necessarily breaking contact gently retreat in the face of her advance.

- Breathe through your nose.
- Close your eyes occasionally so that you can concentrate on how it feels.
- Utter little cries and moans to communicate some of your excitement to your partner.
- Explore the roof of your girlfriend's mouth as well as the inside of her cheeks, her teeth, the region under the tongue, and the tip of her tongue. Your main interest, of course, will be your partner's tongue because it will feel so sinfully soft and will respond to your every move and touch.

Don't:

- Don't be afraid of tongue contact. Some lovers get shy when they encounter their partner's tongue. You must overcome this bashfulness.

- Don't press your lips together because this makes a French kiss impossible.
- Don't extend your tongue too far into your partner's mouth.
- Don't get nervous if you feel your head swimming and your nerves tingling when French-kissing. This is a normal reaction. In fact, if you don't feel these sensations you're doing something wrong.
- Don't overdo it. Many people report that they like French-kissing so much that they do it for an hour or more nonstop. But as with anything else, too much of a good thing can be counterproductive. If you tongue-kiss for an hour without stopping you're bound to decrease your pleasure. The solution is to take a short break every five or ten minutes. Chat with your partner. You might talk about the kiss itself. Have a glass of water or some candy. There's nothing like a French kiss between a peppermint-flavored tongue and a cherry Life Saver–flavored mouth! As you can see, the combinations are endless.

WHAT SHOULD I DO WITH MY HANDS WHILE FRENCH-KISSING?

Although the French kiss involves the tongue, the proper use of the hands is so important to the experience of this kiss that it's fair to say that it is the second most important element of a French kiss. Just as improper use of the hands can ruin a French kiss, sensual hand movements and caresses can make it bliss. Let's begin by examining what to do with your hands above the neck.

Most guys like their partners to gently caress their face while French-kissing. Along the same lines they enjoy it when you play with their hair. You can actually run your fingers through his hair while running your tongue through his mouth. If you do the two together it will feel indescribable. He'll experience a rush of motion inside and outside his mouth. Some guys say it feels like they're in a rocket ship flying through space when a girl does a simultaneous action like that.

If you notice that your guy is getting turned on there's another sophisticated thing you can do with your hands. He's got to be turned on for this to work though. You stick your tongue deep into his mouth like a probe while at the same time gently pulling his hair. Do this in a repeated rhythmic action for a mind-blowing effect. He'll never forget it!

Still another thing women can do is gently hold his ears with your fingertips and tilt his head left and right and up and down in the direction you want while Frenching him. This allows you to control your boyfriend as if he were a pony. This works especially well with tall guys whose heads must constantly be tilted down during kissing. Plus if you're holding his ears and he gives you too much tongue you can pull his ears as a signal for him to slow down and let you breathe.

Guys can try all the above techniques with the added suggestion that if the girl has long hair it's perfectly acceptable to play with it while French-kissing her. Run your hands through her hair as you run your tongue along her tongue.

Another thing girls love is when a guy gently caresses her face with his palms or fingertips while French-kissing.

When your hands move below the neck they can become involved in more erotic caresses and probably one of the most exciting is to hold your girlfriend in your arms like she's a fragile, precious thing. Says one young woman, "It makes me feel protected and loved when he holds me."

Still another thing you can do is run your hands up and down her back while gently moving your tongue in tempo with your hands. If you coordinate this correctly she'll experience a synchronous barrage of sensations that will turn her on much more than either tongue or hand movement alone.

What to do with your hands

- Hug him gently.
- Give him a bear hug.
- Run them up and down his back.
- Caress his face.
- Play with his hair and gently pull it during intense kissing.
- If you know him really well you could pick his pocket.
- Gently hold his ears and tilt his head to the angle that's most comfortable for you.
- Hook your fingers into his belt when doing a sensual kiss and pull him close.
- Rest your hands on his hips.
- Put them around his neck.

How should I snuggle while French-kissing?

Oh young lovers! Here is one of the best parts of French-kissing. You have already learned that tongue contact is heaven, to be sure. But the intimacy of tongue contact calls for—indeed, demands!—a similar intimacy in the position of your bodies while you kiss. This is where advanced technique comes into play.

Once you French-kiss you and your partner will inevitably get really, well—excited. That's the plain and simple truth. And once that happens you can do things together that you wouldn't be able to do at any other time or in any other place, like in a supermarket, say. In other words, tongue contact prepares the way for the snuggling you can do, and the intimate positions of your body will make the French kiss that much more exciting.

The biggest mistake people in the United States make when French-kissing is that they stay too far apart. Kiss like the Europeans. Move closer and draw your partner to you with your arms.

Keep in mind that you can also snuggle while sitting down. There are so many romantic positions to try! One of the best is when you sit side-by-side on a sofa and your hips touch and you turn your upper bodies to face each other and begin to French-kiss. This gives you a chance to caress her face, play with her hair, and cradle her in your arms.

Now that we've covered all this theoretical material, I bet you're ready for some . . . fieldwork. Next time you're with your kissing boyfriend or girlfriend put into practice what you've learned. Then come back and reread this section together to inspire you to try even more French kisses. For if you do them often enough you'll find yourself falling deeper in love than ever before. And after all, *that's* the real purpose of the French kiss.

PART FOUR

The Finer Points of Kissing Technique

The Secrets of Great Kissing Technique

To sum up the theme of this book I'd like to quote a young woman who recalls a meaningful kiss this way: "He kissed so soft and gentle. You could tell he was really paying attention to the kiss itself. He looked deep into my eyes, he caressed my cheek with his hand, he smiled afterward. That kiss was the most romantic experience I have ever had and I'm glad it was with such a nice guy."

Yes, the secret to great kissing technique is connection, passion, and love. Kissing is not merely a prelude to sex—it is fun in and of itself. And with that in mind let's begin our survey of some of the most well-kept secrets of kissing technique.

Looking

The question of whether lovers should kiss with their eyes open or closed is of fundamental importance. It was the question that prompted me to write this book and I'm glad to be able to report some definitive answers here. More than two-thirds of those surveyed preferred to keep their eyes closed while kissing but didn't mind if their partner kept his or hers open. Only one in three likes to kiss with eyes open—and if *your* lover does, you can take it as a compliment. "I prefer kissing with my eyes open unless the girl isn't that pretty," said one twenty-four-year-old.

But you shouldn't worry about your appearance. If your partner kisses with his eyes open, everything will look out of focus. Indeed, because the brain interprets nearby faces as erotic you'll actually appear sexier to your lover when you're mouth to mouth. So open your eyes occasionally and enjoy the view!

"Sometimes the effect of prolonged eye contact is amazing."

"I like eyes open if I'm in love. I like to see my lover's eyes. It makes me feel connected soulfully to him."

"I usually kiss with my eyes closed because it's more romantic. But sometimes I like to peek at my husband because his expression is so tender."

Laughing

Did you ever notice your partner laughing or giggling while kissing? I hope you didn't think they were laughing at you. It simply means they're having fun. The plain fact of the matter is that sexual intimacy produces laughter in many people. Indeed, 87 percent of men and 98 percent of women reported that they sometimes giggled while kissing because of the pleasure they felt. And 2 percent even cried when a kiss felt too good to bear. So if your partner laughs while kissing you know you're doing something *right*.

Phone kissing

Generally a favorite with young people, phone kisses are a vastly underrated form of flirtation between adults. Although the technique simply involves making kissing sounds into the receiver, it can pack an erotic wallop out of all proportion to the ease with which it is produced. Making a kissing noise may sound silly to *you* because you're hearing it in high definition—without the frequency loss caused by telephone transmission—but to your partner it will not only sound like a real kiss but it will *feel* like one too. If you do it right it has all the potential to excite her that a real kiss has and then some. By telling her *where* you're going to kiss her you can fire up her imagination and place kisses wherever you find they tickle her best. Through the power of words and sounds alone you'll excite her more than the greatest lover could with his lips.

MEN:
"I make a smooch sound over the phone. Just smack over the mouthpiece."

"Just a smooch now and then. Most of the time verbal romance via the phone makes me feel awkward."

"You've got to set it up first so her imagination takes over. I start out by saying, 'When I see you I'm going to kiss your belly like this. . . .' Then I come in with the kisses. 'Smack smack smack smack smack smack smack.' Each *smack* is a kiss into the receiver and I don't do them slow, I do them fast one right after the other and I can tell by the way she laughs that she likes it . . . no, she *loves* it!"

"I love nice juicy phone kisses. I have a phone friend I met on the phone from a wrong number. He calls and kisses me without even saying hello and I love it."

"I do it all the time."

"Yes, I explain to whomever exactly how I'm going to kiss them when I get them alone."

"I see my boyfriend only on weekends (he lives fifty miles away) and we talk on the phone every night so we'll often end our conversations with a kiss over the phone."

"Yes. I say, 'Close your eyes. Think of me, take a very deep breath, and let's kiss!'"

Dating

It's wrong to think there's only one right answer to the question of whether you should kiss on a first date. The answer varies from person to person and depends on how you feel during the date itself. Currently, about 85 percent of men and women believe it's okay to kiss on a first date provided you feel comfortable with the person you're dating. The best times to kiss on a date are at the outset when you're just meeting or at the end when you're saying good-night.

The thing to remember is that the kiss will come much more easily if you're on the same wavelength as your date before you attempt it. Keep the conversation going, gaze into each other's eyes for long periods of time, and let the excitement mount between you. Someone once said that if you look into anyone's eyes for five minutes you'll fall in love with them. Plenty of eye contact will make you start to feel like a magnet is drawing you together and after all that romantic attraction a kiss will almost happen by itself.

Kissing Tip

Here are some ideas for when to kiss on a date:

- When you leave a restaurant and you're standing close together trying to decide where to go.
- When at a museum together and you're close and examining a work of art.
- In the middle of the date after you've had a good conversation and have made eye contact for an extended time.
- After you tell a funny joke and you're both laughing together and in a good mood.

Counterkissing

One day I observed two lovers necking on a train. The young woman waited after each kiss before kissing her boyfriend back, gazing dreamily at him for a moment, then leaning forward and kissing him a little lower down on the cheek than he had kissed her. After a while she started peppering him with quick little kisses until he burst out laughing. She was a classic counterkisser.

Counterkissing is a technique rather than a specific kind of kiss. In fact you can counterkiss with just about any type of kiss—a French kiss, a wet kiss, a biting kiss and so on. The object is to wait and see exactly how your lover is kissing you before kissing him or her back. Just as an army can launch various counteroffensives during warfare, you can respond to a kiss with the same general kind of kiss or with a slightly different kiss. Of course, no two kisses are ever exactly alike, but in counterkissing you purposefully become conscious of the type of kiss you're getting so that you can either respond in kind or subtly vary the kiss you've just received. In this way you'll manage to puzzle, amuse, and tantalize your partner. Don't be afraid to tease your lover by taking a long time to kiss back. It's a wonderful form of flirting.

Making up

One of the most delightful pleasures of being in love is getting over a quarrel and making up. Throughout the ages lovers have argued over the silliest things, getting angry and vowing never to see each other again. Then inevitably—sometimes within a matter of minutes—they become reconciled and all their angry emotions are transmuted into the most enraptured devotion. They feel they've never been closer. With your differences ironed out you'll enjoy a new lease on love. Known as *Versöhnungskuss* in German the kiss that marks such a turning point celebrates a special and wonderful experiment in the alchemy of the heart.

There is, however, another side to the make-up kiss. Some people feel it is too easy a solution. One twenty-five-year-old woman says, "I used to kiss and make up, but I won't anymore because my feelings about the kisses (usually really good) mix me up and I shove existing anger back inside me. As a result, after the kiss I feel like I've been corked and can't deal with things further." Another perceptive twenty-year-old woman says, "If the argument is truly resolved make-up kisses are the best in the world. If the argument isn't settled the kiss will let you know."

Moviegoing

Every time I run a kissing survey I find that fewer and fewer people like to kiss at the movies. Maybe as ticket prices go up people just want to get their money's worth by watching the show. Currently only about 25 percent of moviegoers neck during a film. They generally don't like to have people sitting behind them when they kiss. And they usually kiss during romantic or tender moments or when the lights first go down. Kisses in a theater aren't too passionate—they're more likely to be short pecks.

If your partner enjoys kissing at the movies, teach him the copycat game: You kiss whenever the actors do. Of course this works best at romantic films.

WOMEN:

"Generally I don't like doing it when there are people behind me. I've kissed when there are heartwarming scenes, for example families coming together or beautiful scenes of nature. It's close and warm being next to my boyfriend in a dark and nonintimate setting."

"I don't like to kiss but I do love to *grope* at the movies, almost to the point of excruciation!"

"Maybe one or two small kisses in a movie during a romantic or emotional part that we both can relate to."

"I kiss during romantic scenes and hold hands tightly during scary scenes."

"If a movie doesn't hold my attention I feel I might as well enjoy something."

MEN:
"Love to kiss at the flicks. Tend to sit one-third from the front, in the center so we can see. We kiss whenever the fancy strikes."

"It depends on the movie and how much you want to kiss her. A boring movie can make you kiss her immediately. I try not to disturb anyone and sit myself at the back. I hate those heads kissing in the middle of a film."

Driving

Cars are supremely romantic places. You're close. You're in a confined space. And you can drive to scenic and intimate spots. Then there's the whole mystique of lover's lane. In fact, if films and songs are any indication, the link between cars and romance runs long and deep in American and European culture. Not surprisingly 92 percent of people admitted that they enjoyed kissing in a car. Their comments will give you some ideas about when, where, and how to enjoy this thoroughly modern pastime.

"My boyfriend usually drives and when the car is moving I generally give him cheek kisses due to the angle. When the car stops at a light he'll turn his face to me and we'll kiss on the lips. Sometimes we've even kissed on the lips while the car is moving but we do that only when traffic is light."

"When I kiss with a date in a car it usually takes place in the front seat. It's always fun to watch the windows eventually fog up too!"

"I like kissing in a car because it's a small space and you have to make concessions in order to do what you want. It's fun, too, because silly things usually happen."

"It is very uncomfortable having to contort yourself in a car. Note, I don't like sex in the backseat either. If a male does I just pass on by him and tell him to grow up!"

"Car kisses are very exciting and even the chance that someone might see us kissing adds to the excitement."

"Despite the fact that I'm a full-grown adult there's a certain thrill in this—especially parked on a public street. I think I'm a bit of an exhibitionist!"

Greeting kisses

In my opinion the greeting kiss has only one function and that is to pave the way for real kisses to follow. Who knows, but that delectable gal you're air-kissing today may be the girlfriend you're French-kissing tomorrow. Actually greeting kisses are much more common in certain industries like theater, film, and politics, where people are likely to say hello with an air kiss or a kiss to the side of the cheek.

If you don't want to be kissed in greeting, just put out your hand for a handshake instead. But there's nothing to be afraid of because a greeting kiss is never done on the lips. Instead you kiss the air to the side of your kissee's cheek. (Europeans often kiss on one side and then the other.) Make a little smacking noise so they have the pleasure of hearing the kiss. And don't kiss in strictly business environments like offices, courts, banks, restaurant meetings, and auditoriums. Most important, never kiss strangers. The pleasure is reserved for people you already know.

Wearing braces

Does anyone in the world like wearing braces? Apparently not. Most teenage girls with braces are constantly trying to find out how to distract guys from the fact that they're wearing them. But recently I've started hearing that with the growing interest in tongue piercing, braces are coming into their own as a form of jewelry. So if you have braces my advice is to think of them as "mouth jewelry." That way you'll feel more confident and kissable and you'll be more likely to attract partners who will enjoy kissing you.

Mirroring

There you are, the two of you, in all your glory—necking. And as you kiss him you're peeking over your shoulder into a mirror to look at yourself! Mirror kisses are exciting because they let you show yourself off, which satisfies the exhibitionist in all of us, and they let you admire yourself, which satisfies the narcissist in all of us. Twenty percent of lovers have done a mirror kiss and almost all of them enjoyed it. A few got so self-conscious they had to turn away but most people enjoy seeing themselves kissing their partner. "It looked like we were in a movie," says one girl. Another says, "I love it. We're so cute together!" Next time you're in a mirrored elevator with him try kissing until you hear the bell for your floor. Says one girl, "Taking a peek and being able to see ourselves from all angles made it so much hotter."

Turning

Which way do you turn your head when you kiss? Dr. Onur Gunturkun, a German psychologist, actually researched this question for two years, observing one hundred and twenty-four couples kissing in airports and discovering that 65 percent tilt their head to the right. If you and your lover both turn to the right, the good news is you won't bump noses. But if you always turn right you might want to occasionally turn left just to tease her.

"We've read enough!" I can hear some readers clamoring. "We're ready to close the book and kiss!"

And indeed you are, since you've been prepared by thousands of people who have told you what they like about kissing, how they do it, and what it means to them. You know more about the subject than an army of lovers. You're ready to kiss! Find your boyfriend, girlfriend, sweetheart, your soul mate, your honey, your sugar pie, your darling and pucker up! And when your lover gasps in delight and breaks off from a passionate embrace demanding that you admit where you learned to kiss like the gods of love themselves, merely contain your chuckle of triumph, smile to yourself, candidly point to your copy of this book, and prepare to revel in the sensual pleasures that belong to all who have mastered the art of kissing.

$\mathcal{I}$NDEX

ABOUT THE AUTHOR

William Cane is the pen name of Michael Christian. Educated at Boston College Law School, where he served as editor of *The Boston College International and Comparative Law Review,* he practiced law briefly in 1986 before switching careers. He taught English at Boston College for fourteen years and today is a frequent lecturer at colleges and universities across the country. He lives in Jersey City, New Jersey.